The Purpose-Guided Student

DREAM TO SUCCEED

The Purpose-Guided Student

DREAM TO SUCCEED

Jerry A. Pattengale

Boston   Burr Ridge, IL   Dubuque, IA   New York   San Francisco   St. Louis
Bangkok   Bogotá   Caracas   Kuala Lumpur   Lisbon   London   Madrid   Mexico City
Milan   Montreal   New Delhi   Santiago   Seoul   Singapore   Sydney   Taipei   Toronto

ISBN   978-0-07-352241-8
MHID 0-07-352241-4

Publisher: *Kenneth Kasee*
Vice president/Editor in chief: *Elizabeth Haefele*
Vice president/Director of marketing: *John E. Biernat*
Director of Development, Business Careers: *Sarah Wood*
Marketing manager: *Keari Green*
Lead media producer: *Damian Moshak*
Director, Editing/Design/Production: *Jess Ann Kosic*
Project manager: *Christine M. Demma*
Senior production supervisor: *Janean A. Utley*
Designer: *Marianna Kinigakis*
Senior photo research coordinator: *Jeremy Cheshareck*
Photo researcher: *Teri Stratford*
Media developmental editor: *William Mulford*
Media project manager: *Mark A. S. Dierker*
Cover & interior design: *Jenny El-Shamy*
Typeface: *11/13 Minion*
Compositor: *Laserwords Private Limited*
Printer: *R. R. Donnelley*
Cover credit: *© Frank Whitney/Getty Images*
Photo Credits: *Part 1: Mel Curtis/Getty Images/DIL; Chapter 1: © Corbis/Punchstock/DIL; Chapter 2 © Library of Congress/DIL; Part 2 Ryan McVay/Getty Images/DIL; Chapter 4: page 74 © Superstock, Inc., page 75 Reunion des Musees Nationaux/Art Resource, NY; Chapter 6: © Superstock, Inc.; Part 3: Stockbyte/Punchstock/DIL.*

Library of Congress Cataloging-in-Publication Data
Pattengale, Jerry A.
     The purpose-guided student : dream to succeed / Jerry A. Pattengale.
         p. cm.
     Includes index.
     ISBN-13: 978-0-07-352241-8 (alk. paper)
     ISBN-10: 0-07-352241-4 (alk. paper)
     1. College student orientation. 2. College students—Life skills guides. 3. Education,
     Higher—Aims and objectives. 4. Success. I. Title.
     LB2343.3.P375 2010
378.1'98—dc22
                                                                              2008047774

www.mhhe.com

Dedication

Dedicated to Wayne Seybold and Terry Franson, who have demonstrated the value of a Life Wedge for both themselves and their communities. Wayne's journey inspired a city and then a nation—and continues to do so. He grew up in a trailer park in Marion, Indiana, and traveled two hours a day for more than a decade to practice ice skating with his sister, Kim. They stole the hearts of the nation with their success at the 1988 Calgary Olympics, and Wayne won further respect from his home city by returning to become mayor and helping create the Marion miracle—practicing bipartisan politics while reviving a town that is now excelling. Terry Franson continues to use his humble leadership style to develop hundreds of college students into leaders. In spite of his voice problems, he rose high in the ranks of national track coaches and has also trained numerous Olympians. A decade ago, instead of pursuing even higher positions at larger universities, he stepped aside and let his "students" take over as he remains true to his Life Wedge's purpose of developing people. In the process, he simultaneously helped build a remarkable university in Azusa, California.

A shout out also goes to Charlie Johnson who has helped many IUPUI students to realize dreams stronger than their struggles.

About the Author

Jerry Pattengale loves life and continues to pursue it with gusto. At 16 years old, he found himself both a high school graduate and homeless, but he soon found a great temporary home in a college dorm, and education has made all the difference. In a sense, he never left campus—and believes that ideas and dreams have consequences. His recent little book, *Why I Teach* (McGraw-Hill, 2009), captures much of this passion, and his strategies have helped hundreds of universities and their students. Most days, you'll find Jerry at the local Starbucks at 5:00 AM, writing his newspaper column or meeting with students, or you might find him on the Indiana Wesleyan University campus at a student gathering, listening to music he likely doesn't understand but knows is somehow important to his love of communicating with students.

He has a renaissance spirit, with a rich background in ancient history and a national presence in teaching, learning, and student success issues. His Odyssey in Egypt program reached millions of viewers and became a top 10 Web site globally, and his Virtual Advising Link program led the way for online pictorial directories. He coedited the first book on sophomore issues, Visible Solutions for Invisible Students (National Resource Center, USC, 2000), and is coauthoring another, Helping Sophomores Succeed: Understanding and Improving the Second-Year Experience (Jossey-Bass, in press). Jerry has received the "National Student Advocate Award," "NACADA Merit Award," an NEH fellowship to Greece, campuswide "Outstanding Faculty" awards, and various local, state, and regional appointments. He recently served on the national board for The National Resource Center for the First-Year Experience and Students in Transition (USC) and participated in roundtable meetings at the White House. Among his other commitments, Jerry serves on the advisory board for Veriana Networks, Inc., a next-generation media group; the Governor's Council for Faith-Based and Community Initiatives; and the advisory board for The Collegiate Employment Research Institute (Michigan State University).

In addition to appearing on national broadcasts and at a variety of institutes and conferences, Jerry continues to speak to a wide array of campuses. His publications range from a popular newsprint series and the *Accidental Author* (Paxton Media) to research-based texts and articles. He also continues to contribute in his area of history (e.g., *A History of World Civilizations* [2010], *A Brief Guide to Objective Inquiry* [2007], *Straight Talk: Clear Answers about Today's Christianity* [2nd ed., 2008], and a section in *The Light of Discovery: Studies in Honor of Edwin M. Yamauchi* [2007]).

Jerry led the development of Indiana Wesleyan University's (IWU) first-year experience program, centered on a new liberal arts course, "Becoming World Changers." Retention and graduation rates rose more than 20 percent in response. In 2004, IWU received national recognition for these efforts through its selection as a Founding Institution in the Foundations of Excellence program of the National Policy Center (Brevard, NC).

In addition to his student success series for Magna Publications (e.g., *The Teaching Professor*) and PaperClips Communications, Jerry has been a keynote speaker at conferences ranging from the College Personnel Association Conference for Arkansas and the Teaching Academic Survival Skills Conference (TASS) to the Indiana Pathways Conference and the Modern Medievalism Conference. You'll find Jerry's comments in the forewords to the well-received *Student Development in the First College Year: A Primer for College Educators* (USC) and *Shedding Light on Sophomores* (USC).

His Ph.D. is in ancient history from Miami University (OH), where he also earned an M.A. in Tudor-Stuart history. He has another M.A. from Wheaton College (IL) in Interpersonal Development and a B.S. from Indiana Wesleyan University in History.

Jerry's mantra is "The Dream Needs to Be Stronger Than the Struggle," a theme you'll find discussed in this book.

Acknowledgments

The Purpose-Guided Student began during the summer before 9/11, after which its concepts and lessons suddenly gathered widespread interest. However, capturing them in book form for the national audience took nearly a decade of refining and feedback, as well as the efforts of a wonderful team at McGraw-Hill. Linda Schreiber's efforts helped launch this project, and Director of Development Sarah Wood, my editor, helped bring this book to fruition. They have both become colleagues, and their indefatigable nature is greatly appreciated. I'm also encouraged by the strong support of John Biernat, the Vice President for Marketing, who attended conferences at opposite corners of the nation to learn firsthand about this book's importance to the teaching enterprise. He believes in the Life Wedge concept and clearly has been successful at his. I'm also blessed to work with Christine Demma, whose passion for this book nearly rivals that for our beloved Chicago Cubbies. Keari Green continues to help new students and professors discover this text, and Anna Kinigakis's design work is amazing. Also, cheers to William Mulford, Randall King, Paul Crisp, Nathaniel Johnson, and Kyle Hufford for the creative media aspects.

Special thanks to my editor, Eric Ratinoff, who spent long days in New Hampshire poring over this manuscript and countless hours discussing it with me—oftentimes while traveling to campuses to discuss the very lessons you'll find within. Also, a special thanks to his wife Nicole and her reading group near St. Anselm College for being a sounding board for us before and during the review process; the same appreciation goes to Brad Garner, Phil Gardner, Bill Millard, David Riggs, Todd Ream, Don Sprowl, Vanetta Bratcher, Karen Roorbach, Bud Bence, Mike Boston, Terry Munday, Karl Gauby, and Cindy Pattengale for listening to various concepts and, in many cases, experimenting with their applications. Alleta Tippey, my administrative assistant, has been invaluable in helping me with the logistics of countless trips and projects related to the book's theme. My president, Henry Smith, and my provost, David Wright, continue to be rather supportive. I could not have asked for a better working situation, and I wish the same for all of you reading this.

I would also be remiss if I were not to thank those who have funded research projects that have helped with the background of this manuscript: Ball Brothers Foundation; Lilly Endowment, Inc.; and Lumina Foundation for Education. And I'm indebted to Ben Johnston and the nearly 300 representatives from McGraw-Hill who are carrying this book to offices and meetings, not only to solicit readers but also because they believe in its content.

Preface

If we were having coffee for the first time to discuss your college and career plans, it would not be long before I'd draw a "V" on a napkin and begin to ask about your "Life Wedge." That is: "What are you passionate about?" and "Do you sense that your commitments are helping to get you where you hope to go?" Okay, and then the big question: "Where is your life headed?" Like a wedge for chopping wood, I'd note that the sharper and narrower your Life Wedge, the more successful you'll be in reaching your goals. "Do you know the top five time commitments that mainly fill up your Life Wedge?" I'd ask. We'd then jot them in the "V," and then I'd say, "If you continue to do these, will you reach your goal?" If not, "What changes do you think you need to make?" Yeah, you might look at me a little bit funny, especially when you thought we were just going to chat about your class schedule, roommate, or home situation—the typical talk with a new professor. Oftentimes students immediately note that they do not have a main goal or a "purpose" that could serve right now as a target for their Wedge—ah, and that's a great beginning. In the book ahead, we'll look at your Life Wedge in that context, and within a few chapters, we will have a clearer understanding of where your Wedge is headed. Likewise, we'll look at the types of commitments you need inside your Wedge to reach your goal or fulfill what you might consider your life purpose.

Through the years, many students have e-mailed or called me to share something like, "Hey, Professor, let me tell you about my Life Wedge!" or "Dr. P., I know I graduated years ago, but could we meet to talk about my Life Wedge?" Usually, the latter type of conversation is about a major job decision or an opportunity that will take the person's life in a different direction (i.e., point his or her Wedge in a slightly different direction—oftentimes, closer to the cause he or she really wanted to pursue from the early days of college).

Before we'd leave the table, I'd share the following mantra: "The dream needs to be stronger than the struggle." Although a clear Life Wedge and reasonably aligned activities are important, ultimately it is our passion for the purpose or target of our Wedge that sustains us—no matter how well we plan. We all have our struggles, and obstacles can range from the mundane to all-encompassing scenarios. Having a well-conceived dream and Life Wedge, one that is attached to noble ends, will lead to a more fulfilling life and, in the process, a more successful college career.

I would be remiss not to share the beginning stages of this book, before you begin to read it in earnest. As I have traveled the country, providing workshops for colleges large and small on the subject of "student success" and "student motivation," I came to realize that more than 90 percent of the more than 400 colleges I surveyed focused very little on the types of things I just mentioned. Many had robust programs that indeed were necessary and very helpful, but they focused more on keeping students satisfied with their college experience rather than on identifying and pursuing students' life purposes or goals. They focused on the external instead of the internal. Most colleges provide rather important help in the areas of student support such as note taking, time management, and reading skills, but these areas are often detached from any semblance of the students' Life Wedges. It is not an either/or proposition, that is, a focus on skills or on life purpose. Rather, we need to give attention to both. We need to begin with questions about your life purpose—what will eventually motivate you to succeed, while simultaneously building your skills and talents to reach those goals.

A few months after drafting some of the key chapters of this book came the horrendous morning of 9/11.

Most people born before 1992 have rather clear memories of where they were when they learned of the terrorist strikes. Whether people were 10 or 100 years old, they likely have vivid memories of seeing the terrible images for the first time or watching the second building collapse on live television. For me, the day after was also memorable—and it relates directly to one of the chapters in this book. I stood before my class of nearly 200 new students to give a lecture printed weeks earlier in the syllabus schedule: "September 12, 2001: Heroes and Noble Causes."

As you might imagine, this day was indeed different, but the topic could not have been timelier. The room was packed with visitors, from concerned friends of those enrolled to various media personnel. I was still as stunned as my students about what had happened, and yet we found ourselves together for a scheduled teaching moment. Life went on, even when many lives had just been lost and others were still trapped beneath the New York rubble. It was surrealistic. Professors and teachers across the world were trying to find connections with their scheduled lectures, even though the life lessons, sorrow, and concern were sometimes overwhelming.

In that crowded room, we unpacked the basic differences between noble and ignoble causes, how to come to choices about such matters, and the motivational value of attaching our best energies to worthwhile causes about which we are passionate. By looking at heroes' beliefs and decisions, we were able to frame the discussion and begin to chart some common characteristics among the causes we selected as noble, as well as common character traits of our heroes. The key lesson had a direct application to students' college experience: If you are passionate about a cause, you are likely to be motivated. And students who develop an overriding passion for a cause are more likely to succeed than those without such interests.

We were able to use a simple Life Wedge diagram to explain this point and to chart our heroes' actions and pursuits along with our own. If we think of our commitments in terms of a Life Wedge, such that those that are most important drive toward a target, then it is easier to keep our priorities in perspective. In fact, it can prove invaluable in striving for goals.

During our next class, we discussed the "Crossroads Principle," or when events cross our lives' paths, and how such encounters help shape our views and give us direction. Although many of these intersections might seem uneventful at the time, they provide reference points recalled years later. Others, like 9/11, are shared intersections held in common for generations. Almost unanswerable questions emerged on that particular day—"How would you have reacted if you were at the World Trade Center on 9/11?" and "How will your life be different having had such a catastrophic event intersect with your world?" Events like 9/11 cross our paths without any decision on our part. Others can be much more intentional or for positive reasons. We will look more closely at these events in the chapters ahead.

Of course, the tough part about motivation is staying motivated. We can get distracted by more than the big obstacles. We also can be distracted by experiencing a sort of "vertigo" or imbalance. We will consider the different ways we become more easily distracted, as well as a plan for ways to remain aware of these encounters. There is a way to be proactive instead of reactive.

Throughout the text, you'll be asked to write down your reflections, moving from the "Big Picture" to your picture, gleaning insights from a larger discussion to inform your Life Wedge. One of the toughest aspects of college can be finding connections between a current assignment and your future. Sometimes it might be a stretch to see any connection, but usually we can find them. Some of the assignments will be especially helpful with this aspect.

The Purpose-Guided Student is about you, and it's about a purpose of your choosing … a purpose that will guide you, motivate you, and, if all goes well, a purpose that will benefit from you. Education in its purest form is never just about the learners but about the learners' contribution to something greater than themselves.

Jerry Pattengale, Ph.D.

Brief Table of Contents

Table of Contents

Part 3   A Purpose-Guided Plan

1

The Life Wedge

A photograph can connect then and now while celebrating the journey itself.

Forced to face the naked truth

IT REALLY ALL BOILS DOWN TO ONE'S 'DONATION' IN LIFE*

She answered the door naked. It was an awkward moment for my youngest brother and me. She was over 80.

We had come to mow our new neighbor's yard, but that didn't seem important to her just then. Instead, she thrust open the door, grabbed my arm, and pulled me inside. My brother, affixed to my other arm like a parasite, followed suit.

She directed us to sit on the couch, and, still in shock, we obeyed. When she disappeared into the other room, my brother pressed his hand tightly against his baby-toothed grin and tried to control his giggles. I offered a kick in the shin to help him.

When she returned, she placed two bowls of ice cream in front of us, then sat down across the room to pull on her stockings. The plain vanilla scoops were a welcome relief from the awkwardness, and I focused intently on eating that ice cream slower than I had ever eaten any-thing before. Still, out of the corner of my eye, I caught her performing a sort of geriatric hop as she navigated her way into her girdle.

She disappeared several times more, returning each time with a new piece of clothing. While she buttoned, we nibbled on tiny spoonfuls, trying to make the ice cream last until she was fully clothed.

Finally dressed in a mismatched outfit, a wig perched on her head, she sat between us on the couch and guided us through an album of old photographs. Inside, the 80-year-old woman sitting next to us was nowhere to be found; instead, we saw black-and-white snapshots of a gorgeous woman, flanked by business executives, dressed in wools, silks, and other exotic materials completely foreign to two cotton-clad boys from Buck Creek. If not for the matching gap between her front teeth, I would never have guessed that the goddess in those pictures and the loose-skinned lady hobbling around that musty house were the same person.

When she opened the door, I wanted to run away from the woman who was our new neighbor, but when she cracked that photo album, I wanted to know the woman who inhabited those photos—the successful world traveler, the stately career woman, the well-kept woman with the porcelain skin. Where had she gone? It was as if she had taken life's bus from the center of the world to the farthest reaches of oblivion, where she'd become our neighbor.

Today, years later, I still think about that lawn-mowing job. I sometimes ask myself, "Decades down the road, will I answer the door naked?" and "Will young neighbor kids not yet born find me delusional?" and "Will I one day be a stranger in my own land?" The question that grips me most, though, is this: "Am I striving for goals today that I'll discover matter little when I reach life's twilight?"

That twilight may come at 99, as it did for my great-grandmother, or it may come "mid-life," as it did for my father. Although most of us would prefer a long life, Catherine Marshall offers a valuable perspective on longevity in her book, *A Man Called Peter*, about her husband Peter Marshall, the U.S. Senate Chaplain who passed too soon. "It's not one's duration in life that matters," Marshall writes, "it's one's donation."

Lisa Beamer, wife of Todd Beamer, one of the heroes of September 11, reflects on her husband's early passing in her book *Let's Roll*. She relates that on his office inbox, Todd had taped the well-known quote from Theodore Roosevelt: "The credit belongs to the man who is actually in the arena . . . Who strives valiantly, who knows the great enthusiasms, the great devotions, and spends himself in worthy causes. Who, at best, knows the triumph of high achievement and who, at worst, if he fails, fails while daring greatly so that his place shall never be with those cold and timid souls who know neither victory nor defeat." His duration in life was far too brief, but he put himself in the arena, and his donation was enormous.

I occasionally read Martin Luther King's "I've Been to the Mountaintop" speech, which he delivered the evening before his assassination. After expressing gratitude for great civil rights gains, he said, "Well, I don't know what will happen now. We've got some difficult days ahead. But it doesn't matter with me now. Because I've been to the mountaintop. And I don't mind. Like anybody, I would like to live a long life. Longevity has its place. But I'm not concerned about that now. . . ."

From Marshall and Roosevelt to King and Beamer, and from our aging neighbors, too, we learn that we should give first-rate priorities to first-rate causes. One day, whether we're giving our last address to a Senate floor, staring down a terrorist, delivering our own "Mountaintop" speech, or dipping ice cream naked, we'll have expended our life's best energies.

We'll all look back at life's photos and either smile or glance away. My neighbor saw something in her pictures that framed her life's fulfillment. That gaze in her eyes erupted into a smile—a beacon of pride.

In retrospect, I witnessed a royal moment. In our youth, we're distracted by nakedness, however innocent. As we mature, we should be more preoccupied with the naked truth, whatever it may reveal.

AUTHOR'S COMMENTS

I received a flood of comments after a version of this article appeared in the *Chicago Tribune* (on March 4, 2003, used here with permission). I wish I had space to share all of the hilarious stories—and also the touching memories. One of the funniest calls I received was from a dear friend, Katie Beaver, the 90-year-old matriarch of our church, whose husband served as its first pastor. She stood around five feet tall, with a baritone laugh that would fill any room. Katie announced on the phone: "Jerry, this is Katie. I read your article." She paused, and I began to sweat. Then she blurted out, "Just wanted to let you know I still have my clothes on! . . . Gotcha!" Then she burst into laughter.

But she also paused again to say thanks and reflected a bit on her own personal journey. When she passed away a few years later, all who knew her knew she had lived a full and rich life.

QUESTIONS

1. Have you had an awkward or unique experience like that of the naked lady?

2. When you hear people reflect on their lives, what types of things do they seem to find the most joy in talking about?

3. What lesson can you take from the naked lady story that applies to your own life?

4. If you live to be 80 years old, what fulfilling memory would you like to see framed in your living room?

*Jerry Pattengale. *Chicago Tribune* (March 4, 2003): Section 1:13.

1 Dreams: Drawing Your Life Wedge

Splitting Wood

When I was growing up in Buck Creek, Indiana, winter meant splitting wood. We heated our house with a wood-burning stove, and when I became old enough, it was my job to split logs into the firewood that would keep us all warm.

My father used his ax to cut downed trees into logs, but he wouldn't let me use the ax to split the logs. I was too small, he explained, and the ax was too heavy and too sharp. "Besides," he said, "the ax sticks too easily in the wood. Go find yourself a good wedge, and use the sledge."

I don't think that sledgehammer was any lighter than the ax, but at least my fingers were safe. So, with those instructions, I set out to find myself a good wedge.

My father had accumulated quite a collection of wedges over the years, and I experimented with a few of them—different shapes, different sizes, different materials. Each one had a different effect on the log, and on me. If the wedge wasn't sharp enough, or if it was too wide, I could beat on it all day with that sledgehammer and hardly get it through the wood. With enough time and sweat, I could get the log split eventually, but I'd expend an awful lot of energy doing it, and the split wouldn't be very good.

After that first day of log splitting, I was ready to quit. My hands were blistered, my arms ached, and I'd managed to split all of three logs in four hours. But my father would hear none of it. "You'll figure it out," he told me. "Find yourself a good wedge."

The next day, I was back at it. Trial and error taught me which wedges worked best with which kinds of wood, but I finally learned that ultimately, the sharper and narrower the wedge I used, the easier it was for me to split wood. With each day, I got better at matching the right wedge to the right log, and I got better and faster at splitting the wood. Pretty soon, I started looking forward to the days when I had to split wood—I was having fun with it!

I still remember the day my father came over after an especially great day of splitting. A pile of firewood as high as my thigh stood perfectly split and stacked beside the chop block.

"Did you split all of those?" he asked.
I nodded and smiled.
"Today?"
I beamed. I had found myself a good wedge.

Why College?

Now you know how to split wood. But what, you may be wondering, does splitting wood have to do with college, or with being a motivated student?

The sarcastic answer is that unless you get motivated about being a college student, you better start learning how to split wood if you want to stay warm in the winter. But that's not the serious answer.

However, before we get to the serious answer, we have to answer another question first: Why college?

The Practical Reason: Earning Power

All college students have their own personal reasons for going to college. For many, the decision is financially driven: They go to college to earn more money than they could without a degree.

Research by the National Center for Education Statistics shows a direct correlation between earning a college degree and increasing your earning power. In fact, in a 2005 study, they found that the median annual earnings of full-time, full-year workers between the ages of 25–34 years with only a high school diploma were $26,800, whereas the median annual earnings for the same group with a bachelor's degree or higher were $43,100—a difference of $16,300.

That difference might not sound like much. But start multiplying it. Over a 30-year career, that average difference adds up to $489,000—almost half a million dollars! And that's assuming those income figures never change. When you factor in inflation, plus the raises and promotions that a degree might help you qualify for, the difference could be significantly greater over your lifetime.

Looking at those numbers, it's easy to see why someone might view college as a path to greater financial success. Choices you make now, such as what classes you will take, how hard you will work in them, the major you will select, and the basic decision to see college through to graduation, can impact your future financial status, including everything from the kinds of restaurants where you'll be able to eat to the car you drive to the kind of house and neighborhood in which you live.

Just being a college student is a financial decision. For all students, it's an expensive venture—even if you're on scholarship. There are numerous costs associated with college, from tuition and fees to room and board to books and computers. There is also an opportunity cost: You are sacrificing many years from your working life! But when you think about the potential earning power you may gain with a college degree, it's easier to see your education as not an expense but an investment, in yourself and in your future.

Figure 1.1   Salary Survey Based on Educational Levels

Year	All Education Levels	High School Diploma or GED	Bachelor's Degree or Higher

Median annual earnings of all full-time, full-year wage and salary workers ages 25–34 years, by sex and educational attainment: Selected years, 1980–2004 (In constant 2004 dollars)

Year	All Education Levels	High School Diploma or GED	Bachelor's Degree or Higher
Male			
1980	$40,600	$38,800	$46,300
1985	39,100	35,200	48,200
1990	36,700	32,000	46,000
1995	34,200	29,700	46,400
2000	37,800	32,300	50,900
2001	37,600	31,400	51,200
2002	37,300	31,100	51,400
2003	36,600	31,000	49,600
2004	36,300	30,400	50,700
Female			
1980	$27,600	$25,500	$34,100
1985	29,100	25,000	36,900
1990	28,900	23,700	38,800
1995	27,500	21,800	37,300
2000	30,100	23,500	39,900
2001	31,200	24,200	40,200
2002	31,600	24,600	42,000
2003	31,500	24,400	41,300
2004	31,000	24,000	40,300

SOURCE: U.S. Department of Education, National Center for Education Statistics (2006). *The Condition of Education 2006* (NCES 2006–071), Table 22-1. See http://nces.ed.gov/fastfacts/display.asp?id=77.

The Personal Reason: Interests and Passions

Maybe you're not motivated by financial concerns. Maybe you're in college because of a special interest or passion that you have. Perhaps you've always been fascinated by bridges and structures, and you want to learn civil engineering. Maybe you've always admired your teachers and want to pursue a degree in education. Possibly you have a passion for helping the environment, and you're in college to study biology, or ecology, or even political science. Or maybe numbers have always been your thing, and you think a career in accounting or the actuarial sciences might be for you.

Regardless of your interest or passion, college is where you can turn that interest or passion into a career. Through classes, labs, and internships, you'll learn about the subject at the highest levels and find out if that path is a good fit for you. Many students enter college interested in pursuing one subject and find themselves more interested in a new subject they discover by taking a class that sounded interesting. Others find that upon closer examination, they're not as interested in a subject as they thought they were and switch paths, while still others find ways to combine new interests with the passions that motivated them to come to college in the first place.

While focus is certainly an important skill to learn in college, being open to new ideas, classes, and subjects will help you learn which career path is right for you and will make you a well-rounded thinker and learner, which will serve you the rest of your life.

The Other Reason: Finding Your Way

What if you've gotten to this point in the chapter, and you don't really have a financial motivation for being at college, and you don't exactly have a driving interest or passion either? What if you came to college because that's what your friends were doing, or because your parents pressured you to go to college, or because it seems like that's just what you're supposed to do after high school, or simply because you just don't feel ready to jump into the "real world"?

That's okay, too.

While many students enter college confident in their choice of major and career, many more enter college unsure of where it will take them. And while many of those students who arrive at college with their plan all mapped out do follow through on that path, many head in another—or several other—directions before finding their way to the podium at graduation. So if you're not sure exactly what your reason is for being in college, don't worry. You're there to figure out what's next for you—to find your way.

Fortunately, a college campus is a great place to find your way. It's filled with interesting classes, professors, and fellow students who will challenge the way you think, push you to prove yourself through hard work, help you learn how to learn, and open your eyes to new perspectives. College also brings opportunities to get involved in social groups and service groups and to make friends from a diverse student body.

Even if you have no idea what major you will choose, a college education can be a transformative experience and a solid foundation for success, no matter what your path or how winding that path may be.

Journal Entry: Your Reason for College

Throughout the course of this book, you'll be asked to make journal entries. Keeping a journal and writing in it regularly is a helpful way to personalize what you learn, to remember major concepts, to think more deeply about the information that's been discussed in the book or in class, and to keep a record of the evolution of your thinking over a period of time. If you find journaling as useful and valuable as I have, you may feel inspired to write in your journal beyond the assigned journal entries. If so, go for it! The more you journal, the more you will get out of the journaling process, and the more helpful your journal will become.

Essentially, a journal is any place where you record your thoughts about a topic. Today, many people journal publicly through blogging, while many still journal privately in notebooks or on their computers.

I encourage you to keep a journal that is dedicated to this class exclusively, but the type of journal you keep is up to you—some people prefer a notebook that they can carry with them and write in with pen or pencil, while others prefer to type their thoughts rather than handwrite them, and so keep their journal on a computer, either in a word-processing document or in a public or private blog online. Whatever method you choose, be sure that you can access your journal easily and often.

Once you've decided how you will keep your journal, take a few moments to complete the following exercises for your first journal entry.

1. Make a list of the top three reasons you came to college. (Leave space in your journal below each reason.)

2. Next to each reason, rate, on a scale of 1–10, how much this reason motivates you to succeed in college.

3. Below each reason, write a few sentences to explain why you are motivated by that reason.

The Dream

Now let's take a step back from thinking about why you're in college for a moment. (Don't worry, we'll get to wood chopping soon enough.)

Let's think bigger than college, bigger than your first job out of college, bigger than your first apartment or your first car. Let's think about *the dream*.

What is the dream?

Although the mention of "dreams" often conjures visions of fantasy, dreams can be associated with your personal fortune. Who do you want to be when you grow up? What kind of life do you want to lead? What is your dream job? The answers to these questions might seem disconnected from your day-to-day activities, but your ability to dream—to envision clearly an ideal future that inspires and excites you—can help you find the motivation to act and make the decisions that will lead you toward the rich and full life you imagine.

The Making of Dreams

Dreams, and dreamers, often get a bad rap in today's society. Dreamers are often portrayed as hopeless romantics with their heads in the clouds, out of touch with reality. But where would we be without dreamers and their dreams? The great American poet Carl Sandburg once wrote, "Nothing happens unless first a dream." Indeed, almost every great institution and invention we enjoy today, nearly every victory of social justice, every scientific breakthrough, every artistic triumph, and every athletic championship began with a dream.

The true power of dreams is their ability to give you a guided passion. No matter your academic or economic background, guided passion—a motivation to work toward achieving your dreams—can help provide you with the focus and drive you need to succeed, in college and in life. In fact, research shows that students who have a general understanding of their life purpose (and, in turn, the purpose of their education) are much more likely to succeed in college. Those students are also likely to develop a viable plan for a career path—one that will provide earning power as well as personal fulfillment.[1]

Understanding Dreams and Dreammaking

You may have never sat down with pen and paper and formally "dreamed," but certainly you've had wide-awake dreams at some point in your life. Maybe they were just fleeting daydreams, or maybe they were detailed and involved. Maybe you dreamed of something you just hoped might happen, or maybe you dreamed of something you believed would happen if you worked for it.

Examining dreams you've already dreamed can help you develop new dreams. Take a few moments now to think about things you've dreamed about in the past. In the grid below, write down the first three dreams that come to mind that you've dreamed about in the past. Then, in the middle column, write down if the dream came true (if it still might, you can write "not yet"). Finally, in the right-hand column, if the dream came true, write why you think it did, or if it did not, why you think it did not.

Figure 1.2   **Dream Grid**

Past Dreams:	Came True?	Why or Why Not?
1.		
2.		
3.		

Mature Dreams vs. Immature Dreams

Now I'd like you to look at those dreams you wrote down through another lens: maturity.

The maturity of a dream—whether it's an immature dream or a mature dream—is not determined by how old you are when you dream it. Rather, the maturity of a dream is determined by how serious you are about pursuing it, how willing you are to act on it, and, indeed, whether or not you have acted on it already.

---

[1] A 2005 study conducted jointly by Indiana University and Indiana Wesleyan University reveals that an intentional curricular program designed to help students determine their life purpose correlates with radically higher graduation rates. (Leaders of the research team include Drs. Edward St. John [University of Michigan], Don Hossler and Jeff McKinney [Indiana University], and Jerry Pattengale and Bill Millard [Indiana Wesleyan University].)

In other words, an ***immature dream*** is just wishful thinking, but a ***mature dream*** is one that puts passion into action.

Seen through this lens, the maturity of a dream is then not only about the dream but also the dreamer.

Let me give you an example. Thanks to the early rounds of *American Idol* auditions, every new season brings us a reminder of the thousands of people who think they have what it takes to be pop stars but are, for all intents and purposes, tone deaf. Think about the people who are subjected to ridicule in those early rounds: They sing off key, they don't know the words, and they ultimately embarrass themselves because they look like they've never sung into a microphone before.

When they walk into that audition room, they have a dream—becoming the next American Idol. But if they have no experience singing other than in their cars with the radio turned all the way up, if they've never taken a single voice lesson, and if they've never performed in front of a live audience, their dream is immature. It sure would be nice if it came true, but it's not very likely.

The *American Idol* finalists, however, are another story altogether. Take Kelly Clarkson, the winner of the first season of the show in 2002. Kelly started singing in the school choir in seventh grade. She sang in shows and musicals throughout high school. She had classical voice training. She wrote dozens of her own songs. When she walked into that audition room, she had a dream, too—a mature dream that she'd been working toward, in measured steps, for years. When her opportunity came, she was ready.

Journal Entry: The Maturity of Your Dreams

Now that you understand the difference between a mature dream and an immature dream, take a look back at the three dreams you wrote down in the previous exercise. Would you categorize them as mature or immature? Mark either an "M" or an "I" next to the dream in the column on the left to indicate whether you think the dream is mature or immature.

Next, look at the column on the right—the why or why not column. Think about what you wrote there in terms of mature dreams versus immature dreams. How does the maturity or immaturity of the dream relate to why the dream has come true or not? Take a few moments to write your thoughts in your journal.

In Defense of Immature Dreams

I want to clarify a few things before we move forward: First, it's perfectly all right to dream immature dreams. They're fun to dream, and there's no harm in, say, imagining what you might do if you won the lottery. Immature dreams can also help you develop your imagination, a valuable skill that can prove helpful when you focus it on pursuing a mature dream. That imagination that you've sharpened dreaming immature dreams might help you find a creative solution that will lead to the achievement of a mature dream. So go ahead and dream those dreams. Just remember they're not the only kind, and don't expect that simply dreaming them will make them come true.

Second, immature dreams don't have to stay immature forever: They can grow up and turn into mature dreams. Let's say, for example, that ever since you were a kid, you've loved fast cars and powerful engines, and you want to be an automotive engineer. You declare engineering as your major as a freshman, and you're ready for the fast track. However, you fail your first semester of college math.

Does this mean the dream of being an engineer is over? No.

But shouldn't you be able not just to pass, but excel at math to be an engineer? Well, yes.

So how is that not the end of the dream?

Well, it's the end of the immature dream. It's time for you to either give up on that immature dream or force it to grow up. It's time to reexamine that dream and see if you understand what it takes to make it a reality and decide if you are willing to put in the work necessary to pursue it. If you're willing to take that math class again, and study twice or perhaps three times as much as you did before, and you're willing to get a tutor for the class and meet with the professor during office hours and do your homework with a study group so that you not only pass the class but master the concepts taught in it, and you're willing to put in that kind of work for the math and engineering classes that will follow, that immature dream just might grow up.

If you're not willing to do those things, maybe you just like fast cars. You can always watch car races on TV.

What I'm trying to say is, a setback is just a setback. Don't let it kill your dream. Instead, let that setback be the wake-up call you need to help that dream mature.

Pursuing Mature Dreams

Helping an immature dream grow up is one way to dream a mature dream. But that can be a bit of a long route to get to a mature dream. Let's take a more direct route.

Think now about what *you* really like to do—the things that make you get out of bed in the morning, that quicken your pulse, that make you smile, that give you hope. Whether you are 19 or 49, if you can begin to understand what fulfills you, you're more likely to choose dreams that match up with what motivates you. Thinking about it in the context of college, having the right dreams for you can help you choose the right major for you, which can help you find connections with your assignments, which can help you find the motivation and energy to do them well, all of which can ultimately help you to stay in school through to graduation.

Journal Entry: Dreaming Mature Dreams

Here it is: your invitation to dream a little dream. In your journal, take a few moments to think about two dreams: a personal dream and a professional dream. The personal dream can be about your family, your dream house, or a trip you've always wanted to take. The professional dream can be about your dream job, starting your own company, teaching high school, or being featured on the front page of the newspaper.

Below each dream, write down how mature that dream is right now and explain why. How much thought have you put into that dream? How much research have you done into what is needed to accomplish it, and how much research needs to be done? How detailed is your plan for achieving that dream, and what still needs to be planned?

Even if the dream is not especially mature at the moment, take some time to help it grow up a bit. Think about the things you will need to do to accomplish each dream, and write them down.

The Struggle

How do you feel about those dreams you just wrote down? Is it exciting to see them on paper? Writing out your dreams not only helps you remember and visualize them, it can also be the first step to achieving them. I know when I write down my dreams, they feel more real, and I feel like I'm on my way.

Then I remind myself that writing my dreams down is the first step, not the last. Between those steps, between you and the attainment of your dreams, lie many challenges. Accomplishing most dreams requires hard work, patience, persistence, sacrifice, and incredible commitment. On the way, you're likely to face setbacks, suffering, and loss. Perhaps you'll doubt yourself. Perhaps you'll doubt your dream.

No matter what obstacles you face on your way to realizing your dream, you won't be alone. Few dreams are ever handed to anybody on a silver platter. Achieving most dreams requires a struggle.

I think that's a good thing. The tougher the struggle, and the more you have to prove yourself, the more you will learn and grow on the way, and the more you will appreciate the dream once you get there. Ultimately, though, if you're going to get there, the dream must be stronger than the struggle.

I'm going to repeat that, because it's a key concept to this book:

The dream must be stronger than the struggle.

Stronger Dreams

What makes a dream strong—strong enough to overcome the struggle? Believe it or not, you've already taken the first step in making your dream strong: You've written it down. Seeing the dream clearly is critical to achieving it. That means not only dreaming it but being able to visualize it, being able to articulate it to yourself and others, and writing it down.

Once you're clear about what you want, you have to think about what it will take to get there. You need a plan. To develop that plan, start by asking yourself the following questions:

- What steps do I need to take to achieve this dream?

- When do I need to take those steps?

- What resources (financial, personal, physical, etc.) do I need?

- What skills do I need to achieve my dream?

- How many of those skills do I currently possess?

- Which skills do I need to develop?

- Where can I learn and practice these skills?

- Would a mentor (or multiple mentors) help me achieve my dream?

- If so, do I have that mentor? Have I talked with my mentor about my dream?

- If not, where can I find a mentor? How soon do I need to identify one?

- Who else besides a mentor can help me achieve my dream?

- Have I told these people about my dream? Have I asked for their help?

- What obstacles might I encounter on the way to the dream?

- How do I plan to overcome those obstacles?

The more of these questions you can answer, the stronger your dream will become. Even if you don't know a lot of the answers to these questions right now, you do know what you need to do first—find the answers to these questions. Your search for answers may take you to the library, to your professors or advisors, friends, bosses, or family members. As you gather answers, information, and resources and develop your plan, remember that the more detailed the dream, the more real it will become to you, and the closer you will be to achieving it.

Of course, a plan is not a guarantee of success. New businesses are a perfect example of this. While we often hear about the successful start-ups and the entrepreneurs who founded their business in a garage and turned it into a multimillion-dollar company, the number of new businesses that fail annually is daunting—even ones with sound business plans. Hong Kong, long considered a prize international marketplace, averaged 15,884 bankruptcies annually during 2001–2006.[2] We can only assume that most of these were serious endeavors, mature dreams backed by considerable planning.

While planning can't overcome every obstacle, it is still the critical first step in pursuing any dream.

Journal Entry: Developing a Plan

In your journal, go back to the personal and professional dreams you wrote down earlier. On a new page, write one of those dreams (personal or professional, your choice) at the top of the page. Below it, answer as many of the questions in the section above as you can. Brainstorm ideas that you will need for your plan, and identify the details you know and the information you will need to find. For the latter, write down where you will look or with whom you might talk to gather that information.

Once you've completed that exercise for the first dream, take a few minutes to go through the same process with the second dream. You'll develop these plans further at the end of the chapter.

---

[2]Official Receiver's Office: The Office of the Hong Kong Special Administrative Region; see www.oro.gov.hk/cgi-bin/oro/stat. cgi?stat_type=W&start_year=1989&end_year=2007&end_month=2&Search=Search.

The Motivation of Mature Dreams

A plan is critical for accomplishing your dream. Equally important is the motivation to execute that plan.

I believe a prerequisite for finding that motivation is that the dream is your dream. Many people choose majors or even careers to please someone other than themselves—parents, for example. I understand why this happens, but I encourage you to make sure that your dreams are your own. It can be challenging enough to find the energy and motivation to pursue your own dream. If you are following someone else's dream, summoning the motivation may be even more difficult, and you might soon find yourself questioning the time, energy, and effort you're putting forth. With so many things out there that can trip up your dreams and add to the struggle, don't add another one if you can avoid it. Make your dreams your own, so the motivation can be yours as well.

Motivation is key to achieving your dreams because the energy needed to pursue them is significant. Some days you won't feel like doing the hard work. Some days you won't even feel like getting out of bed. Some days you'll think about letting the setbacks win.

Overcoming those setbacks, getting out of bed, doing the hard work—in other words, mustering the energy to achieve your dream—are easier if you have many things motivating you toward accomplishment.

For example, when I was in high school, my dream was to earn a letter in football. My motivation for that dream was mixed. Because I was smaller than most of the other boys, I was driven by an inner or *internal* desire to overcome the odds against a player my size making the team, let alone playing. I was also motivated by an outer desire or *external* reward—to earn that letter and wear it proudly on my jacket. The motivations were linked, as the letter became for me a symbol of the internal goal. Having two motivations to pursue my dream made the dream stronger.

Although we live in an era in which our most precious natural resource, fuel, is becoming more and more scarce, it's exciting to realize that our own reserve of energy is renewable.

Your energy belongs on a short list of "intangible" assets that stays with you wherever you go and that never belongs to anyone else. Combined with your knowledge and skills, your energy is a resource that is invaluable not only in reaching your dreams, but in moving forward civic and humanitarian causes as well.[3]

The late Edward "Chip" Anderson, long-time professor at UCLA and Azusa Pacific University, had a great saying about the impact of motivation on achieving dreams. "If the Why is big enough," he used to say, "the How will show up."[4]

---

[3]This "intangible" concept is introduced in Tim Sanders' *Love Is the Killer App: How to Win Business and Influence Friends* (New York: Random House), 2002.

[4]This statement was commonly shared by the late Edward "Chip" Anderson, long-time professor at UCLA and professor at Azusa Pacific University. He helped to establish Gallup's *StrengthsQuest* program.

Journal Entry: The Motivation Behind Your Dreams

Realizing future aspirations isn't an accidental thing, and neither is finding a life goal or dream. Take a few moments now to examine the motivations behind your aspirations and dreams, to understand better your passion and to assess the strength of those dreams.

In your journal, go back to the plans you wrote out for your personal and professional dreams. Underneath those plans, list your motivations for accomplishing those dreams.

My Dream Come True

This book is part of my dream. Like most dreams, it didn't come true overnight.

I began seeing connections between dreams and accomplishments early in my career, finding patterns that could and should be taught in the college or corporate setting. I conducted research into the phenomenon and began to develop a program using the lessons I learned. I've had the opportunity to share that program with more than 6,000 students, and over an eight-year period, the college that used this program saw the number of students who stayed in school through graduation increase by 20 percent. In other words, by applying the ideas and lessons you're reading in this text, 1,200 more students remained in school. I've seen it myself: Discussion of dreams, life goals, and "life purpose" issues makes a difference.

Of course, the book didn't write itself. It has taken seven years from my first draft until finally seeing this book through to publication. Now that you're holding this book in your hands, you're part of my dream, too—to help college students use the power of dreams, goals, and motivation to succeed in school, and beyond. Thank you.

Honoring Your Dreams: The Drum Principle

A few years ago, after I had just given a speech about the importance of having dreams, a recent high-school graduate named Tad came up to me and excitedly told me about his dream: being a professional drummer.

"That's great, Tad," I said. "How many hours are you practicing a week?"

"Well, Dr. Pattengale," he replied, "I've been really busy working, so I haven't had a chance to practice much lately."

I nodded understandingly, but I was already growing suspicious. "Tell me, Tad," I probed, "What type of drums do you have?"

"Well, Dr. P.," he responded sheepishly, "I'm actually a bit short on money right now, and I had to sell my drums."

"Huh," I said. "Well, I saw you drive in tonight in a new Suburban. Is that yours?"

"Yeah! Do you like it? I've always wanted one, and there's plenty of room in the back for my drum set."

Unfortunately, there wasn't enough room in his wallet for his drum set, and there wasn't enough time in his days to practice. He said his dream was to be a drummer, but he chose to spend his precious hours and dollars on other things.

"I do like it, Tad," I told him. "But it sounds to me like you sold your drummer dream for a gas-guzzling machine that'll be rusted out in a few years."

"Oh, no, Dr. P.," he quickly replied. "I got it rust-proofed."

I smiled. "Well, that's good for your truck," I said. "But is it good for your drumming career? I worry that unless you sell that Suburban and put the money toward a new drum set, you'll never become a drummer."

"Oh, no, Dr. P.," Tad said assuredly, "I just need a little more time to get around to it."

That conversation took place over 20 years ago. Tad never did get around to it; he's still not a drummer. He doesn't have that Suburban anymore, either, but what's worse is that he dropped out of college because he couldn't afford the tuition payments and the car payments. The last I heard, Tad is paying the bills, but unfulfilled in his job.

Maybe Tad never would have become a professional drummer, even if he had sold that Suburban and bought a drum set. But maybe his pursuit of that dream would have led him to another career in music, like being a record producer or studio engineer, teaching music, or helping people through music therapy. Maybe he would have opened a store that sold drum equipment, or maybe he would be writing movie scores and soundtracks. But the choices he made about how to spend his time and money sidetracked him not only from his dream but from all the other opportunities he may have discovered along the way, engaging in what I call the **Drum Principle**.

Then again, maybe Tad could have become a professional drummer. And though he's not as young as he used to be, it's not too late. But unless he rethinks his priorities and his life choices, he'll never know.

Personal Alignment

Am I suggesting that Tad is a bad person, or that Tad is a failure in life? No. I'm not suggesting that Tad's choices—to drop out of school, to buy a nice car, to sell his drum kit—are necessarily bad choices, either. They may be the right choices for some people in some circumstances.

However, those choices were bad choices for Tad's dream of being a professional drummer. And while I haven't had the chance to ask him about it, my guess is that Tad might be disappointed in himself for failing to commit the time and energy necessary to pursue his dream honestly—for failing to make choices that supported his dream.

When your actions match your words, you are practicing **personal alignment**. In other words, the choices you make are aligned with the dream you wish to pursue.

Failing to align your choices with your dreams makes it very difficult to achieve those dreams. Think of a car whose wheels are out of alignment. It's difficult to steer, and whether it pulls to the right or it pulls to the left, you've got to work extra hard just to keep the car out of the ditch and on the road, let alone get it where you want to go.

Pursuing your passion works the same way. If you dream of going to graduate school, but you're choosing to spend time watching TV with friends rather than spending extra time in the library, you may be out of alignment. As you consider decisions, from when and how much to study to which courses you take each term, keep your dreams in mind, and work to align those choices with them.

To give your dream a chance to come true, you need to pay attention to all the small tasks that are connected to that dream. Put another way, *you need to pay serious attention to those tasks connected to a serious dream!*

The Wedge Principle

Remember the wedge? You know, from the wood-splitting story? Let's come back to that now.

Back in Buck Creek, I learned that a sharp, narrow wedge would help me get through the wood and achieve my goal of keeping our house warm faster, and with less wasted effort, than if I used a dull, wide wedge. In an auditorium in the 1970s, I learned that the same principle applies in life.

The speaker, Dr. Keith Drury, took a piece of white chalk and drew a giant "V" on the blackboard. Your life, he explained, is like a wedge.[5] The more narrow it is, and the more sharp and focused its point, the more likely you are to reach your goals.

Unlike my father, Dr. Drury didn't tell me to go find myself a good wedge—he told me to make my life into a good wedge. Here's how he explained it.

First, I had to know my goal. When I was splitting wood, that was defined for me—I wanted to get through the wood so I could heat the house. But much like the kind of wood determined what kind of wedge I should use, Dr. Drury explained that the kind of goal determined what belonged in my wedge. What went "in" the wedge was determined by the choices I made about how to spend my time, and, indeed, my life. I began to understand what he meant: If I knew my goal, and I chose my activities so they were focused on that goal, it would be easier to achieve that goal. But if I filled my wedge with things that were distractions from my goal, the wedge would get too wide, and achieving the goal would take more energy and more time, just like splitting wood with a dull, wide wedge.

This, then, is the essence of the ***Wedge Principle***.

A Closer Look at the Wedge Principle

Let's look at a diagram of a ***Life Wedge***, illustrated in Figure 1-3. Three main components make up the diagram: life purpose, life focus, and life gifts and life skills.

The right wedge achieves the goal efficiently and effectively.

---

[5]Keith Drury is an associate professor at Indiana Wesleyan University.

| Figure 1.3 | **The Wedge Principle** |

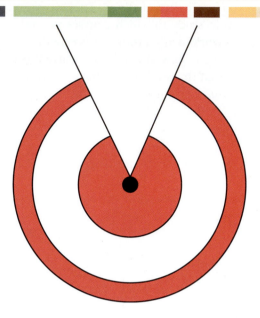

Life Purpose: The Point of the Wedge

A wedge is built for a specific purpose. In wood-splitting, that purpose, like the tool itself, is simple: to split wood. Our Life Wedge is also built for a specific purpose, a purpose we alone decide. Once we identify a life purpose—the point of the wedge in both senses of the word—we can begin to fill our Wedge with the commitments and skills we need to move forward.

To build the right Life Wedge for the right purpose, think about personal alignment, which we discussed previously. Your dream, your major life goal, will help you determine whether you are forming a sensible and promising Life Wedge. You already have written down a personal dream and a professional dream, but perhaps you feel you have a bigger dream, a life purpose to which those other dreams lead. Maybe you have a heightened interest in a cause (e.g., defending human rights, providing equal access to education, curtailing drug traffic in your town) or a special interest in a field or career. If you don't have a driving passion or sense of life purpose right now, that's okay, too—you can apply the Life Wedge to a shorter-term purpose as well, like graduating from college.

Life Focus: The Breadth of the Wedge

If the wedge is too broad, it won't split the wood. Imagine trying to split a section of a tree with a broad wedge. You can take special aim, pound relentlessly for hours, and even skip meals to keep at it, but that wide wedge won't penetrate the wood effectively, so despite all that exertion, you'll still have few results besides blisters at the day's end. Perhaps eventually the effort would force the wedge into the wood and split the tree, but that small success would come at great expense of energy and time.

Unfortunately, that's the way many students approach college: too many clubs, too many social events, too many odd jobs competing with classes . . . each of which makes their Life Wedge wider. For your Wedge to help you reach your goals, it must be narrow and focused enough to drive through challenges and distractions. You must be cautious and deliberate about what you put into your Life Wedge, or your commitments will sap your focus and take away from your effectiveness in achieving your purpose, the point of your Life Wedge.

Think about how you spend your time. Do you invest your time, or do you just "kill" time? How you spend your hours and days—in other words, what you put into your Life Wedge—affects your ability to attain your goals. Thus, you should fill your Wedge with commitments that move you closer to your goal. Not every activity must be focused on your goal, of course. You need to take care of yourself, not just by eating, sleeping, and exercising, but also by spending quality time with friends and family and pursuing hobbies and interests that make you happy. Those will ultimately support the pursuit of your dreams because they will keep you mentally and physically healthy and help you have the mental and physical energy to pursue your goals.

However, to ensure that your Life Wedge is sharp and effective, you need to whittle it down to specifics rather than thinking in broad, general terms. If the goal at the tip of your Wedge is too broad, or what you put into your Wedge is too general, you're going to be like me out there with that wide wedge, trying to split firewood. For your life goal or life purpose, and the corresponding Wedge, think *focus*. As you narrow your definition of what you want in life, you sharpen your Wedge.

Life Gifts and Life Skills: The Sharpness of the Wedge

If the wedge is dull, it takes longer to cut. Our Life Wedge must not only be narrow but sharp. Abraham Lincoln once wrote, "If I had eight hours to chop down a tree, I'd spend six hours sharpening my ax." Imagine attempting to split wood with a wedge that's narrow and focused but rather dull. Once again, more swings are needed to complete the task. Often, a dull wedge can get stuck in the wood, a frustrating setback. A dull, narrow wedge is more effective than a dull, broad wedge, but when you add sharpness to the focus of the narrow wedge, now you're chopping wood.

The sharpness of your Life Wedge is determined by the seriousness with which you pursue the commitments that determine the Wedge's width. The *volume* of what you put in your Wedge determines its focus, but the *quality* of what you put in determines its sharpness. Your natural gifts, talents, personal strengths, learned skills, and educational training all impact sharpness. Reading outside-of-class assignments, attending on-campus lectures, attending study sessions, and meeting with professors during office hours all help keep you (and your Life Wedge) sharp.

Constructing an Instrument Panel

In a sense, the Life Wedge helps us find our bearings and have a clear picture of where we're heading. It can also help you find direction and decrease your sense of confusion, sometimes called feelings of **vertigo**.

Vertigo is a phenomenon frequently experienced by pilots; it refers to a state of imbalance, often described as a sensation of dizziness or whirling around. *Subjective vertigo* is a false sensation of movement in which the person feels he is spinning when he is not, whereas *objective vertigo* is a perception that surrounding objects are moving. Vertigo occurs for a number of reasons: fatigue, moving too quickly, loss of horizon, too much noise and vibration, fixating on one object at the expense of all else, and flickering lights.

Metaphorical vertigo is a phenomenon frequently experienced by modern students (and professors, too). Let's look at how some of the vertigo triggers are experienced in a campus setting and how we might avert them:

Fatigue. Exhaustion dulls our senses and performance; it's not hard for me to tell when someone in my class is dragging. If I see students struggling to stay awake in class, or I notice poor performance, I'll ask questions about their schedule: "Walk me through a normal weekday," or "How long do you spend on the Internet each day?" Using the Life Wedge, we'll then look at their commitments and priorities and discuss how quality rest fits in to that equation.

Moving Too Quickly. We jump into commitments without thinking through the consequences for many reasons: enthusiasm, curiosity, guilt, believing we can do it all. Many students are especially interested in humanitarian service and will often jump headfirst into good works, even if the time commitment negatively impacts other facets of their lives. Before diving into a new commitment, think about your decision-making process. Are you making a decision, or just falling into something? How much time are you giving yourself to consider this decision? What steps did you use to decide? Have you considered the greater good you might do after college by investing more in your Life Wedge commitments right now?

Loss of Horizon. When a student, like a pilot, loses a reference point for direction, the result is often wandering—and sometimes that wandering leads right out of school. If I observe such a lack of focus, I try to reconnect the student to his or her Life Wedge (or prompt the development of one) and link activities and commitments back to the Wedge.

Too Much Noise and Vibration. We can all relate to mental overload, but it's not healthy in any sustained form. As James K. A. Smith, Associate Professor of Philosophy at Calvin College, told me, "In order for me to write I need to get rid of all the chatter." I find that many of today's students, having grown up with e-mail, instant messenger, text messages, and cell phones, not to mention TV, the Internet, iPods, and video games, are so accustomed to constant chatter and distractions that they're unfamiliar with the calming (and focusing) effect of plain old silence. If I sense a student is suffering from chatter overload, I'll ask, "When did you last experience extended quiet?" Sometimes this question gets the student to realize it's been quite a long time and consider the benefits of seeking out a quiet place. We'll also talk about how revisiting her Life Wedge might help bring some perspective to what seems to be a hectic time.

FIXATING ON AN OBJECT AT THE EXPENSE OF ALL ELSE. I've seen students encounter this hazard in numerous situations: in an intense dating relationship, as a member of a sports team in competition season, when making a new commitment to a campus organization, or when discovering a new social scene. In these and other similar cases, I often recommend that students talk with campus counselors when situations feel out of control. But here again, pausing to consider your Life Wedge can be helpful. In many cases, the person doing the fixating doesn't realize it; if you find a friend in one of these situations, you may be able to help by suggesting he take a step back to consider his Wedge.

FLICKERING LIGHTS. Rex Miller likens this cause of vertigo, often from strobe lights or intermittent light seen through helicopter blades, to the "endless noise and vibration of experts on every issue." He adds that "The media compound the problem by bombarding our attention with the flickering strobe light of daily crisis all day, every day."[6] However, if you're going to lean successfuly into your future, you need to concentrate on what Stephen Covey, author of *The Seven Habits of Highly Effective People*, identifies as your sphere of influence. It's easy to get distracted by various crises beyond your control, among roommates, distant relatives, or friends of friends. In these situations, consider how you prioritize your commitments in the light of others' needs and how distractions might keep you from realizing your own dreams. I've found that when a student can move from, "I'm really worried about my roommate" to "I'm going to encourage my roommate to go to student counseling, so I can stop trying to solve all her problems and focus on my studies," both the student and the roommate end up better off for it.

While these examples might seem like minor difficulties that are simply part of the student experience, the consequences of vertigo can be severe. According to author Ed Chinn:

> Those suffering from vertigo lose all sense of vertical and horizontal orientation: they literally lose their alignment to, and placement in, the real world. Pilots suffering vertigo have flown their planes full throttle into the earth.
>
> Because it represents the tyranny of the subjective, the only effective recovery from vertigo is an absolute, resolute, focused reliance on objective reality (such as an airplane instrument panel).[7]

Throughout the years, the Life Wedge has helped many students construct an instrument panel with which they can more calmly and confidently navigate their lives.

---

[6]M. Rex Miller, *The Millennial Matrix: Reclaiming the Past, Reframing the Future of the Church* (San Francisco: Jossey-Bass, 2004), p. 3.

[7]Ed Chinn, quoted in Miller, *The Millennial Matrix*, pp. 2–3; the list of vertigo causes were also gleaned from this insightful section.

Moving Toward Your Ideal Wedge

All this talk about the Life Wedge may make it seem as though all you have to do is scratch one out on a piece of paper and start living it. But as you've probably guessed by now, it's not quite that easy.

You essentially have two versions of your Life Wedge: your **Ideal Wedge** and your **Real Wedge**. Your Ideal Wedge is your Life Wedge as you would like it to be, in an ideal future state, whereas your Real Wedge is the Wedge that reflects how you're actually spending your time and prioritizing your energies right now. Let's compare the two.

Your Ideal Wedge Chart

You've spent time already in this chapter writing about your dreams, your plans, and your motivation. Using these dreams, or a bigger life purpose if you prefer, complete the Ideal Wedge chart with the commitments, activities, relationships, and causes that would go into your Ideal Wedge.

Your Real Wedge Chart

Your Real Wedge chart records what you're actually doing with your time—what you're actually putting into your Wedge at this moment in time. Completing a Real Wedge chart can be extremely valuable in helping you gain perspective on how effective you are and where you might need to sharpen your Wedge to move it closer to your Ideal Wedge. In a sense, a Real Wedge chart is a way

Figure 1.4   Ideal Wedge Chart

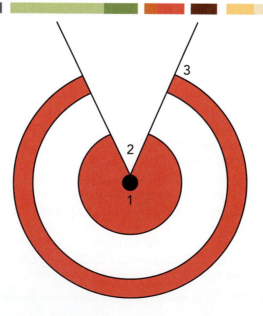

Figure 1.5   Real Wedge Chart

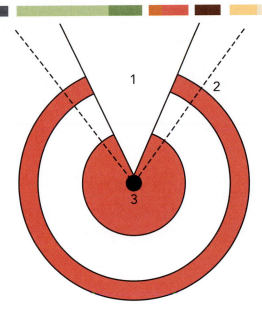

to visualize your current priorities. How these priorities rank in your life determines how close or how far you are to building a path and reaching your life goal.

Complete the Real Wedge chart above, entering the activities, commitments, and priorities on which you currently spend your time and energy. Be honest with yourself—the more accurate a picture your Real Wedge chart is, the more you'll be able to improve upon it.

Closing Thoughts on the Wedge Charts

If your Real Wedge doesn't look very much like your Ideal Wedge right now (and it probably doesn't), don't feel bad. But do understand that if your Real Wedge doesn't start transforming into your Ideal Wedge—if you don't connect your Real Wedge with where you want to go—you're going to have a difficult time making real progress toward your life goals.

Too often, I look at people's Real Wedges, and they are cluttered with things that have nothing to do with moving forward toward their goal. The exercise of completing these two charts can help you identify those things that don't help you move forward and those that do, so you can make smarter decisions about how to spend your time and build yourself the kind of Life Wedge that will be sharp enough, narrow enough, and strong enough to slice through even the toughest struggles as you work toward your dream.

The narrower and sharper your Life Wedge is, the better. You can keep it narrow not only by keeping in it the things that matter but by ensuring that what you put in your Wedge is well articulated and thought through—something to which you are truly committed. For example, you can put a mediocre performance in a class into your Wedge, but it won't strengthen or sharpen that Wedge nearly as much as doing the best you can in that class so that you can take what you learn there and apply it later.

Building your Life Wedge is a lifelong process because you will continually find ways to sharpen the Ideal Wedge, and, in turn, improve the Real Wedge. Also, your major life goal may change several times due to new learning experiences, enhanced personal strengths, or simply accomplishing goals you set earlier. The sooner you make the conscious decision to work on improving your Wedge, the more fully the passions and interests that you put into the Wedge can develop.

To paraphrase the Abraham Lincoln quote, invest time in sharpening your wedge. When it comes time to split wood, you'll have much more success.

Journal Entry: Questions to Help Sharpen Your Wedge

On a daily basis, ask yourself the following questions to help sharpen your Life Wedge. Writing these questions in your journal will help provide a regular reminder.

- Am I spending time on the tasks that narrow my Life Wedge, or widen it?

- What tasks from my Ideal Wedge can I incorporate into my Real Wedge? How?

- What tasks from my Real Wedge are widening or weakening it and distracting me from my goal? What can I do about them?

- If I keep wedging ahead with these priorities, where will I end up?

Chapter 1 Review

SUMMARY OF MAJOR CONCEPTS

- A college education can be a foundation for success, no matter your path.

- Dreams can give you a guided passion and help you find motivation to act.

- An immature dream is just wishful thinking, but a mature dream puts passion into action.

- The dream must be stronger than the struggle.

- "If the Why is big enough, the How will show up."—Professor Edward "Chip" Anderson.

- Pay serious attention to those tasks connected to a serious dream.

- The closer your Real Wedge is to your Ideal Wedge, the more likely you are to reach your dreams.

KEY TERMS

immature dream   a dream about the future that is essentially wishful thinking, with no plan in place to support it.

mature dream   a dream that puts passion into action by developing the plans, strategies, skills, and resources needed to achieve it.

Drum Principle   the principle that states that you need to pay serious attention to those tasks connected to a serious dream.

personal alignment   when your actions match your words, and the choices you make are aligned with the dream you wish to pursue.

Wedge Principle   the principle that states that just as a sharp, narrow wedge is more effective at splitting wood, a sharp, focused life is more effective at helping you reach your goals.

Life Wedge   a visual representation of the Wedge Principle, containing three elements: life purpose, life focus, and life gifts and life skills.

vertigo   a phenomenon that induces a state of imbalance, often described as a sensation of dizziness or whirling around; frequently experienced by pilots.

Ideal Wedge   your Life Wedge as you would like it to be, in an ideal future state.

Real Wedge   the Life Wedge that reflects how you're actually spending your time and prioritizing your energies right now.

APPLICATION EXERCISE 1

Goal Setting

In the journal entry "Developing a Plan" that you completed earlier, you began to answer some of the critical questions that will help you create a plan to achieve your dreams.

While the dream is your *long-term goal*, you will need to reach a series of *short-term* goals along the way.

In the movie *What About Bob?*, Bob (played by Bill Murray) is a paranoid patient struggling to overcome his many fears and phobias. Psychiatrist Dr. Leo Marvin (played by Richard Dreyfus) encourages Bob to take "baby steps" to overcome his fears—to focus on the little things that he can handle rather than the big things that can seem overwhelming. In other words, rather than think about all the things that could go wrong on an elevator ride, he encourages Bob to focus on the small steps (literally) he needs to take to get him into the elevator and start the journey.

While the movie became a cult classic of slapstick comedy, the idea of "baby steps" clicked with millions of viewers. People understood that small, manageable steps line the path to bigger goals, which can seem scary and intimidating if you only look at the end result.

Now let's take some of the items you outlined in your planning process in your journal and turn them into specific short-term goals—baby steps that you can take along the way to your dream. Below, or in your journal, identify three short-term goals that you feel can be accomplished by the end of this academic term. List them below and answer the following questions about them:

Short-Term Goal 1: _____

Target Completion Date: ___/___/___

Evidence that this goal is reached:

Possible steps to reach this goal:

a)

b)

c)

Possible obstacles to reaching this goal:

Resources needed to reach this goal:

a)

b)

c)

Short-Term Goal 2: _____

   Target Completion Date: ____ / ____ / ____

   Evidence that this goal is reached:

   Possible steps to reach this goal:

   a)

   b)

   c)

Possible obstacles to reaching this goal:

Resources needed to reach this goal:

   a)

   b)

   c)

Short-Term Goal 3: _____

   Target Completion Date: ____ / ____ / ____

   Evidence that this goal is reached:

   Possible steps to reach this goal:

   a)

   b)

   c)

Possible obstacles to reaching this goal:

Resources needed to reach this goal:

   a)

   b)

   c)

APPLICATION EXERCISE 2

Tracking Your Week

To know if you're spending your time wisely, you need to know exactly how you're spending it. An effective way to visualize your real priorities—what you're putting in your Real Wedge—is to track the time you spend over a week.

Figure 1.6 is a time-tracking chart you can use to track your hours. However, you may want to create your own version, using a spreadsheet program, that

Figure 1.6   Time Tracking Chart

Wedge Time-Tracking Sheet

Time of Day (M–F)	Monday	Tuesday	Wednesday	Thursday	Friday	List Two Main Time Commitments per Time Bloc	Time of Day (Weekend)	Saturday	Sunday	List Two Main Time Commitments per Time Bloc
7:00 AM to Lunch (___)						1. _____ Amount of time: ___ 2. _____ Amount of time: ___	7:00 AM to Lunch (___)			1. _____ Amount of time: ___ 2. _____ Amount of time: ___
Lunch to Supper (___)						1. _____ Amount of time: ___ 2. _____ Amount of time: ___	Lunch to Supper (___)			1. _____ Amount of time: ___ 2. _____ Amount of time: ___
Supper to 10:00 PM (___)						1. _____ Amount of time: ___ 2. _____ Amount of time: ___	Supper to 10:00 PM (___)			1. _____ Amount of time: ___ 2. _____ Amount of time: ___
10:00 PM to 3:00 AM						1. _____ Amount of time: ___ 2. _____ Amount of time: ___	10:00 PM to 3:00 AM			1. _____ Amount of time: ___ 2. _____ Amount of time: ___

At the end of the week, you'll be able to look at this chart and pick the items that are consuming most of your time. Since your weekends are likely much different than your week-days, these are tracked separately. List the biggest consumers of your time within your Real Wedge—this is where you're actually spending your time. If you're having a difficult time listing anything of significance for a bloc of time, you might track your days literally by the hour. If you are not listing any concrete items, the implication is idle time (put "I"). Add your own abbreviations to simplify your tracking.

reflects the hours you are typically awake during the day. It will also be helpful to keep this chart with you, either on your computer or in your journal, so that you can enter your activities at several points during the day rather than trying to remember your whole day after you get home.

Track your time in reasonable segments (i.e., when you move from one activity to another), and, again, be honest. This tool will help you update your Real Wedge chart later in the book.

REMINDERS

As you consider your Life Wedge, when you sketch "V's" on scrap papers, napkins, and other items, remember that there are two forms—the real and the ideal. The real reflects what you're currently doing and the ideal helps you to envision where you want to be.

2 Heroes and Their Causes

On the Steps of History

"I am happy to join with you today in what will go down in history as the greatest demonstration for freedom in the history of our nation."

With those words, Dr. Martin Luther King Jr. began perhaps the most well-known speech of the twentieth century, his "I Have a Dream" speech.

On August 28, 1963, standing on the steps of the Lincoln Memorial, Dr. King championed the cause of equality and challenged the American people to support the cause of civil rights. He also, famously, talked about his dream:

And so even though we face the difficulties of today and tomorrow, I still have a dream. It is a dream deeply rooted in the American dream.

I have a dream that one day this nation will rise up and live out the true meaning of its creed: "We hold these truths to be self-evident, that all men are created equal."

I have a dream that one day on the red hills of Georgia, the sons of former slaves and the sons of former slave owners will be able to sit down together at the table of brotherhood.

I have a dream that one day even the state of Mississippi, a state sweltering with the heat of injustice, sweltering with the heat of oppression, will be transformed into an oasis of freedom and justice.

I have a dream that my four little children will one day live in a nation where they will not be judged by the color of their skin but by the content of their character.

I have a dream today!

I have a dream that one day, down in Alabama, with its vicious racists, with its governor having his lips dripping with the words of "interposition" and "nullification"—one day right there in Alabama little black boys and black girls will be able to join hands with little white boys and white girls as sisters and brothers.

I have a dream today!

I have a dream that one day every valley shall be exalted, and every hill and mountain shall be made low, the rough places will be made plain, and the crooked places will be made straight; "and the glory of the Lord shall be revealed and all flesh shall see it together."

This is our hope, and this is the faith that I go back to the South with.

Dr. King's speech became a rallying point for supporters of desegregation and the civil rights movement, and less than a year after he gave that speech, the Civil Rights Act of 1964 was passed. That same year, he was awarded the Nobel Peace Prize for his efforts.

Bigger Than a Dream

Though the best-known parts of that speech involve what Dr. King said about his dream, that dream was part of something much bigger—a ***cause***. A cause is an ideal or goal pursued with passion and dedication. In most cases, a cause brings many people together to work toward shared goals, and those efforts in turn affect many others. Some people feel so strongly about a cause that it becomes their life's work.

Dr. King's dream outlined specific examples of racial harmony across the land. He hoped that others would be inspired by these examples and thus be motivated to work even harder in support of the cause of civil rights for all.

When a dream is inspiring enough for you to invest your time and energy in working toward it, you know you have a strong dream. When a dream is inspiring enough for many people to invest their time and energy in working toward it, you have a cause.

Heroes: Championing a Cause

When the cause of civil rights comes up in conversation, Dr. King's name is sure to follow. He committed himself to championing, or actively and vocally supporting, that particular cause. In doing so, he became a hero to millions around the world.

Many of the people we consider heroes earned that respect and admiration because of their success in championing a cause and the impact they have had on the lives of others.

How do heroes come to be associated with their cause? How did these people whom we identify as heroes focus their dreams and, in turn, their energies toward the cause that ultimately came to define them? Perhaps most important, where did they find the motivation that helped them champion that cause, often in the face of great hardships and intimidating challenges?

In the case of Dr. King, you could argue that he was born to his cause: He was born into segregation and experienced its sting every day of his life. However, while millions of others also were born to that oppression, not all of them took up the cause in a way that made them national heroes. Yet the civil rights movement is a perfect example of a cause that brings many people together. While Dr. King is probably the most recognizable face of the civil rights movement, countless others contributed their energies, their time, and, in some instances, their lives to the cause—including many individuals who were not directly discriminated against but still chose to cast their lot with the cause of civil rights. Dr. King became the most vocal and visible leader of the cause, which helped establish him as a hero of the movement.

Sometimes heroes take up a cause because the cause finds them. Lance Armstrong earned the respect and admiration of the sports world for his cycling victories in the Tour de France, which he won seven consecutive times from 1999 to 2005. But people consider him a hero today because of his efforts toward the cause of fighting cancer. It's certainly possible that Armstrong would have supported that cause regardless of personal circumstance; many people have lost friends and family members to cancer or know someone who has beaten cancer and contribute time or resources to cancer-related causes.

But Armstrong chose to become more than just a supporter in the fight against cancer. Motivated by his personal experience overcoming testicular cancer, he took a leadership role in establishing the Lance Armstrong Foundation. Because of his dedicated efforts, and because of his media presence and those millions of yellow wristbands, his effort produced amazing results. His tireless support of his foundation's cause of uniting, inspiring, and empowering people affected by cancer prompted millions of people who never once saw Armstrong compete in the Tour de France to consider him a hero.

In both of these cases, personal experience—specifically, personal hardships—provided the motivation for these heroes to work tirelessly in support of their cause. However, not all causes are championed by heroes as well known as Martin Luther King Jr. or Lance Armstrong, and in many cases, the motivation for pursuing the cause comes not from personal struggle but simply from a passion to make a difference.

For example, you've probably never heard of Millard Fuller, but I'll bet you've heard of his cause. Unfulfilled by the millions he made in the marketing industry, Fuller walked away from the business he had founded and instead chose to commit himself to the cause of building "simple, decent, affordable houses" with—and for—those who lack adequate shelter. He empowered thousands of volunteers across the globe to support his cause through the organization he founded in 1976 to support it: Habitat for Humanity International.

Though you may have never heard the name Millard Fuller before that last paragraph, he is nevertheless a true hero to the people whose lives have been impacted by the cause he has championed.

Journal Entry: Identifying Your Heroes

In this section, we've briefly discussed the concept of causes and identified some individuals who have earned recognition as heroes because of the cause they have championed. Take a few moments now to identify some of your personal heroes. Try to list at least five people whom you consider heroes, and write their names in your journal.

Then, next to each name, identify the causes associated with them, if applicable. The cause doesn't have to be well-known; what's important in this journal entry is thinking about what your heroes have committed themselves to in their lives.

Next, after you have identified the causes for your heroes, take a few moments to write down some of the personal qualities and characteristics that you admire in your heroes, and write those in your journal.

Finally, make note of any similar traits among your heroes by circling any characteristics or qualities that you listed at least twice.

DEFINING A HERO

Consider the qualities you circled in your listing of heroic characteristics. Are those common to all heroes? Are there other characteristics common to many heroes that did not make your list? Take a moment to compare your list of heroes, causes, and characteristics with a classmate's list. What similarities do you find? What about differences?

In recent years, *The Harris Poll, U.S. News & World Report,* and *Time* magazine have all invited people to submit their choices for heroes and define the characteristics common to heroes. Many respondents stated that heroes don't give up until a goal is accomplished, they do the right thing regardless of personal consequences, and they go above and beyond peoples' expectations.

In response to the *Harris Interactive Survey, U.S. News & World Report* came up with the following list of qualities of heroes based on responses to their own survey. Take a look at the list and identify the similarities and differences between this list and your list, as well as the lists of your classmates.

1. They go beyond the call of duty.

2. They act wisely under pressure.

3. They risk their life, their fortune, or their reputation.

4. They champion a good cause.

5. They serve as a calling to our higher selves.

Harris Interactive Poll #40 "America's Heroes" (August 15, 2001). Also visit www.harrisinteractive.com/harris_poll/index.asp?PID=251. *U.S. News & World Report,* August 20, 2001.

If you're like me, you'll agree that the qualities in this list would serve any hero—or for that matter, any person—well. You'll also probably agree that there are probably as many definitions of heroic qualities as there are examples of heroes. What's important here is getting you thinking about your heroes and how they came to be who they became. While heroes may not always set out to be heroes, they rarely become heroes by accident.

A Foundation in Values

While a dream often serves as inspiration for a cause, encouraging people to reach for the stars, a successful cause also needs a strong foundation. For most successful causes, shared ***values*** provide that foundation. Values are time-tested principles that help guide decisions and behavior.

Looking at the example of Dr. King, we can see numerous values shared by supporters of the cause of civil rights: fairness, equality, justice, and non-violence. Those values came to define the civil rights movement and helped provide direction, guidance, and strength for supporters of the cause, even when things were difficult. Because their efforts were rooted in those values, and because they believed those values were both important and right, they confidently believed that their cause, which championed those values, was also important and right.

Noble and Ignoble Causes

Most people would agree that the examples of causes we've discussed thus far—civil rights, fighting cancer, and working to provide adequate housing for all—are ***noble causes***. But what makes a cause noble? Is a cause noble by definition?

As we've just discussed, values are at the foundation of any cause. However, values alone do not make a cause noble. Think for a second about where the term "values" comes from. Value is a measure of the worth we place on something, through words and deeds. For example, if fairness is important to you, if it has great worth to you, then you value it, and you could say fairness is one of your values. But if accumulating financial wealth is important to you, even if you must negatively impact others to increase your wealth, then clearly you value wealth . . . and others might say that greed is one of your values. As you can see, values can be positive or negative—and between fairness and greed on the values spectrum, there is plenty of room for debate.

Noble causes, though, are generally acknowledged to be founded on honorable values and qualities. ***Ignoble causes***, to the contrary, are generally acknowledged to be founded on dishonorable values and qualities.

This distinction raises another question: Who gets to judge what is honorable or dishonorable? Who says what is noble or ignoble? Certainly, every society and religion makes these judgments. As individuals, we judge the nobility of causes by deciding which we will support and which we will not. And, of course, history judges the nobility of causes as well.

Let's look at the civil rights movement as an example again. Today, most everyone would agree that it was a noble cause, grounded in honorable values. And yet, for many years, the efforts of that cause were opposed. While history now judges the cause of opposing civil rights as an ignoble cause, those who supported that cause—those who actively fought against the civil rights movement—did not see themselves in the wrong at the time. They chose to support a cause we now call ignoble because they, too, strongly believed in a set of values. However, the values they struggled for were different from the values of those who struggled for fairness, equality, justice, and nonviolence.

It's easy to look back through history and find leaders whose causes we now judge as ignoble and whose values we now judge as dishonorable. But the reason their names are in the history books is because at that historical point in time, many people supported those ignoble causes and shared those dishonorable values.

How, then, do you judge a cause or a set of values without the benefit of hindsight? Sometimes that may be an easy question—for certain causes or values, the way you were raised, the laws and ethics of society, or your own conscience may make the answer clear. But there will be times when the answer is not so easy. Part of the struggle we talked about in the last chapter involves not shying away from difficult decisions but instead weighing different options, considering all angles, and debating the merits of your potential choices. By giving serious thought to these matters, you assure that you do not champion a cause carelessly or promote values lightly.

Of course, you can argue that if you go through all the steps we've discussed, and ask yourself those tough questions, and still decide to support values or pursue a cause that others deem "ignoble," you have the right to pursue such a cause. This is true. If you make that choice, it's also your responsibility to accept the consequences that might come from pursuing such a cause. Before committing to a cause, ask yourself what values underpin the movement and whether those values might be in tension with commonly held values and beliefs.

Rating Importance of Causes

A significant waste of resources	Definitely unimportant	Appears to be unimportant	Somewhat Important	Definitely Important	An optimum use of resources
Only causes at least "definitely important" & "definitely positive" can also be "noble"					

Rating Nobility of Causes

Ignoble	Definitely negative	Somewhat negative	Somewhat positive	Definitely Positive	Noble
Only causes at least "definitely negative" & "definitely important" are usually considered "ignoble"					

Journal Entry: Examining Your Heroes' Values

Earlier, you identified five personal heroes, the causes associated with them, and some of their personal qualities and characteristics that you admire.

Now, go back to that list and try to identify some of the values that were important to each of your heroes. Try to think of at least three values for each of your heroes.

Then, look back at the list of causes and characteristics. For each of your heroes, write down how you think their values connected with and supported their causes and their character.

From Values to Character

What do values have to do with achieving your dream or, for that matter, with being a motivated student?

In your journal entry, you may have discovered that some of your heroes' outstanding qualities were *manifestations of their personal values*. For example, perhaps you identified selflessness as a characteristic of one of your heroes and noted that your hero strongly believed in the values of respect for others and human equality. Oftentimes, there is a direct link between someone's values and his or her *character*.

Below is a list of personal qualities—traits most people would call examples of strong character. As you read through the list, think about your heroes and others you may not yet have considered. Next to the traits, write down the names of heroes who exhibited these personal qualities. Did those qualities position that hero to be selected for a cause? As you work down the list, think again about the connections between character, values, heroes, and causes.

Examples of Personal Qualities

Characteristics a person manifests in his or her actions

On the left are suggestions that appear in numerous lists. Next to each one, write the name of a hero who you think possesses this quality. You will likely have various names on the right side, and feel free to list more than one name per quality. In this exercise you might think of an effective leader in an important local cause or an influential community person as the "hero." Or you might stay with the list of heroes that have already come to mind. Also, many heroes also have negative qualities; list a few at the bottom of the chart (which appears on the next page).

Positive Qualities (Author's suggestions)	Heroes who possess them
Bold	_____
Confident	_____
Cooperative	_____
Creative	_____
Critical Thinking	_____
Focused	_____
Honest	_____
Humble	_____
Observant	_____
Optimistic	_____
Patient	_____
Perseverant	_____
Selfless	_____
Teachable	_____
Wise	_____

Additional Positive Qualities
    (Your suggestions)

Hero who possesses them

_____   _____
_____   _____
_____   _____
_____   _____
_____   _____
_____   _____
_____   _____

Negative Qualities (Your suggestions)

Hero who possesses them

_____   _____
_____   _____
_____   _____
_____   _____
_____   _____
_____   _____
_____   _____

Journal Entry: Examining Your Values

In the last chapter, you had the opportunity to dream big dreams, think about what you want to accomplish in life, and examine why you're here at college. Now let's approach those issues from a different angle: your values.

As we've discussed throughout this section, values form a foundation for causes and dreams and therefore can impact how and where you choose to invest your energies. Taking time to give serious thought to your values will help you make thoughtful choices about what belongs in your Life Wedge and may help you identify a cause or causes that you wish to pursue.

In examining the civil rights movement, we identified fairness, equality, justice, and nonviolence as values that helped define the cause and determine choices and actions. In your journal, take a few minutes to identify the values that are most important to you. Then, pick three of those values, and for each one, write down how that value connects to your dream or to a cause you would like to pursue.

Actions: The Courage of Conviction

All this talk of values, causes, and dreams sounds pretty wonderful, doesn't it? But you and I both know that talk is the easy part—it's action that makes it happen. So how does action fit into this equation?

In the last section, we talked about values helping guide decisions and behavior. And in the last chapter, we talked about *personal alignment*, or matching up the choices you make with the dream you want to achieve.

Let's expand that definition of alignment here: The more a cause is aligned with an inspiring dream above it and rooted in solid, timeless values below it, the stronger the cause will be, and the greater chance it has of success. Just as a dream must be stronger than the struggle, a cause must be stronger than the struggle as well—in many cases, the struggle faced by those pursuing a cause can be even more intimidating than the struggle faced by one person chasing a dream.

No matter how aligned a dream may be with a cause and values, aligning actions with those values is critical for advancing the cause and achieving the dream. And that's where it gets tough.

Here again, examples from the civil rights movement serve as excellent illustrations of the point. Think about some of the best-known stories from that struggle: Rosa Parks refusing to move to the back of the bus in Montgomery, Alabama, in 1955; the nine students who integrated Little Rock Central High School in Arkansas, despite opposition from the governor, in 1957; and the college students who staged lunch-counter sit-ins in Greensboro, North Carolina, in 1960.

In each case, the people involved—Rosa Parks; the high school students, who came to be known as the "Little Rock Nine"; President Eisenhower, who called in federal troops to assure compliance for those high school students; the college students whom the restaurant would not serve—chose their actions based on their personal values, which aligned with the values of the cause of civil rights: fairness, equality, justice, and nonviolence.

Not one of those actions was easy to choose. Each act took courage. In each situation, it would have been much easier just to keep quiet—to accept the injustice, to accept the unfairness, to accept the inequality, and to not make a big deal.

But those individuals didn't want what was easy; they wanted what they believed was right. And because they had the courage to act in accordance with their values, to prove that those values were more than just nice-sounding words, they advanced the cause one step closer toward the dream.

To put it the way we discussed during the last chapter, *they paid serious attention to the tasks and actions connected to a serious dream.*

Walking the Talk: A Daily Challenge

Actions are an important part of this discussion because actions are where the idealism of dreams, causes, and values becomes reality. You can declare your belief in the loftiest values and swear your support to the noblest causes, but if your actions do not align with your words—if you don't walk the talk—even the most honorable words will ring hollow.

However, I'm assuming that, like me, you're not perfect, which means that while we strive to meet the high standards of the values, causes, and dreams we proclaim, we will sometimes fall short. We may truly value personal responsibility and accountability yet still act irresponsibly; we may talk about the importance of personal discipline, and yet still struggle actually to *be* disciplined. And that's okay: We're not perfect. What's important is that we keep trying, every day, to align our actions with our values. That process—of challenge, struggle, failure, and growth—is critical to the development of our character.

The wonderful reality of character is that it's not programmed into our DNA. It's something we impact and develop every day. That presents a tremendous opportunity and daunting challenges—to walk the talk, to make decisions and choose actions that align with our values, and to support the causes and dreams in which we believe.

Journal Entry: Learning from the Struggle

Take a moment to think about a time when your actions did not align with your values. In your journal, write down what happened, and why: What were your values, and what was the action that conflicted with those values? Why do you think you chose that action? Were there consequences of acting in a way that did not align with your values? Finally, and perhaps most important, write down what you learned from that incident, and how that incident helped shape your character and future decision making.

Causes and College Students

Often when I discuss causes, one brave student will stop me and say, "Causes are great, but I'm worried about survival—passing my classes, paying my bills, graduating, and hopefully finding a job. A cause would be a luxury." In other words, causes are nice, but really, who has the time?

Other students tell me that they're too young and inexperienced to choose a cause and that they want to wait until they've graduated and are out in the "real world" before making big decisions like that.

Perhaps you're nodding your head in agreement with one—or both—of those sentiments. If so, I understand where you're coming from. After all, I began college more by default than by design, not giving much thought to what my future might hold. I simply followed a couple of friends, and suddenly I was a college student. I certainly wasn't thinking about causes.

In response to concerns about time and survival, I don't mean to encourage you to devote yourself to a cause at the expense of important things like school-work or your career. I do mean to encourage you to remain open to things that will enable you to live life more richly than simply working to pay the bills—and to appreciate that college is an ideal time to consider causes that might align with your passions. I know many people who were introduced as students to a cause that has now become their life's work.

As far as fears of picking a cause prematurely, choosing a cause now doesn't mean that you can't also choose to support other causes that matter to you later in life. However, taking the time now to invest yourself in a cause, even a little bit, will help you develop a better understanding of what it might mean to take up a cause in later years. In some cases, people support a cause in college only to discover that the cause is not where their passion lies. These students are usually happy to make this realization sooner rather than later.

Ultimately, you don't need to complete this course knowing what your cause in life is—that's not the intent of the discussion of causes. Rather, my hope is that this chapter will help you become aware of and alert to causes, which will make you receptive to embracing a cause when you encounter one that is a good fit for your Life Wedge.

And because I have seen how well a sharp, narrow Life Wedge supports people who are passionate about a cause, I think discussing causes in the context of the Life Wedge will make you more prepared to align a cause with your Wedge.

Gaining by Giving

What drives people to get involved in a cause in the first place?

For most individuals, the motivation is simple: They want to make a difference. And because a cause enlists the support of so many people, and because a cause is often so wide-ranging, there are lots of roles you can play in supporting a cause. Even if you don't have the knowledge, experience, or skills to be a leader of a movement, by pooling your resources with the other people who care about that cause, your contribution can make a greater impact.

If you do see yourself as a leader, a cause presents an opportunity for others to join forces with you and climb on board in support of your efforts. It's incredibly affirming to find that other people feel the way you do about a cause and are willing to work with you in support of it.

Through working with others toward a cause, you will undoubtedly learn and grow. You might learn how large organizations work, or you might simply become more educated about the issue that is central to the cause. You also might learn specific skills such as event planning, financial management, or public speaking.

Pursuing a cause you deem worthy or noble often stems from an ***intrinsic motivation***, an internal drive that reflects genuine interest. (***Extrinsic motivation***, in contrast, might be motivation inspired by external rewards or praise.) Individuals who commit to causes due to intrinsic motivation are more likely to succeed at tasks considered helpful in pursuing those noble causes. As a bonus, the skills you gain in pursuit of a noble cause also can help you in many other areas of your life.

As you develop these skills and work with others toward a common purpose, you also will expand your professional network and interact with others who can serve as mentors and friends who can help you in your career. Perhaps one day, you will find someone to mentor you through a cause you both share.

Getting involved in a cause also can provide direction and focus to your energies and efforts. I have found that any student who begins to pursue a noble cause and then finds a link between that cause and his or her education is likely to graduate.

Finding Your Cause

Though we've used heroes as examples to talk about causes, causes are not the private domain of heroes or people you read about in the history books. Anyone and everyone can find his or her own cause and contribute to it. But how do you find your cause? Why should you devote your energies to it? And how does a cause fit into your Life Wedge?

Let's start with the first question: finding your cause. Earlier, we discussed how sometimes a cause can find you, as it did with Lance Armstrong and Martin Luther King. Of course, even if a cause finds you, you have to make the choice to act. Many people are affected by cancer but choose to focus their energies on their recovery, and there is certainly nothing wrong with that. But many who are touched by cancer want to do more than just beat it personally—they want to support others who are fighting cancer; they want to help raise money to support research into cancer-fighting treatments and drugs; or they want to raise awareness of testings, screenings, and other preventive measures that can help people stop cancer before it starts.

If there is an issue that affects you personally, your cause may have found you. If not, one way to identify a cause that might interest you is to look to your values. Perhaps your values or your personal dream connects to a powerful cause.

Another consideration might be your personal strengths, skills, and interests. You might never have thought about adult literacy education as a cause that you would support, but if you excel in English class, you love to read, and you enjoy helping people one-on-one, perhaps this is a cause you should consider. If you have played organized baseball or softball at the high school or college level and love the game, you might explore supporting the cause of Major League Baseball's Reviving Baseball in Inner Cities (RBI) program, which is designed to provide playing opportunities for inner-city youth, increase the self-esteem of disadvantaged children, and encourage kids to stay in school. No matter your skills or strengths, there is likely a cause that would benefit from your knowledge and experience and would appreciate your time and energy.

When considering causes, remember that not every cause will catch the national spotlight like some of the ones we have discussed here. Many causes are small, local movements—but the impact they make on communities and the lives of the people in them are no less significant. Smaller, more local causes may also provide you with a greater opportunity to have a direct impact on the success of the effort.

Remember also that though you may choose one primary cause to which you lend your energy and effort, your support is not limited to one cause. Even if your resources are limited, you can find many ways to support the different causes you believe in: making a financial donation, volunteering your time, casting a vote, or lending your voice, through a signature on a petition, presence at a demonstration, or other visible endorsement.

If you've ever received a phone call asking for a donation or a solicitation in the mail, you know that in today's society there are many worthy, noble causes, all of which would greatly appreciate your support. Your challenge is to identify the causes that matter most to you and to decide to get behind them.

Journal Entry: Causes to Consider

We've looked at several ways to identify causes that might be right for you. Using the criteria we discussed in the previous section, identify at least five causes that interest you, and write them in your journal. Next to each cause, write down why that cause might be a good fit for you. If you don't know a specific organization or movement, you can write down something more general, like "helping homeless children" or "saving wetland ecosystems."

Below that list, write down three skills, strengths, or experiences you have that might make you well-suited to supporting a cause, and write down the cause you think matches up with those skills, strengths, or experience. If the cause you write down is the same or similar to one of the five you identified in the first section, make a note of it.

Preparing to Succeed: Connecting Your Cause to Your Wedge

Throughout this chapter, we've examined heroes, their causes, and their character, and we've also looked at the connections between a cause, a dream, values, and actions. Now let's take the next step and connect these things to your personal Life Wedge.

As we discussed in the first chapter, your ideal Life Wedge is a reflection of what you value and what is important to you. Your dreams and major life goals help determine the commitments and activities that go into your Life Wedge. When you include the topics we've discussed in this chapter, you can see the bigger picture of that Life Wedge and how dreams and goals can link with causes and values. Ultimately, the more thought you give to all of these aspects, the more precise your Ideal Wedge will be.

Of course, the challenge is getting your Real Wedge closer to your Ideal Wedge—to tie your cause, dreams, values, and goals to actions, behaviors, and decisions; to walk the talk; and to have your time commitments, your activities, the money you spend, and the choices you make align with where you want to go and who you want to be.

If you've given yourself ample time to think and reflect as you've completed the journal entries in this chapter (rather than rushing through them just to get them done), you've already done some significant work on your Life Wedge. You've thought about your personal heroes and why you admire them; you've examined their values and how those values connected to their causes and their character; you've looked at your own values and how those values connect to your dream and your character; you've thought about personal alignment between values and actions; and you've begun to consider causes that might be worthy of your life's work, as well as ones that fit your personal passions and strengths. That's some heavy stuff—and it will all help you develop a stronger, sharper Wedge.

The next step is to draw more direct lines between your causes and your actions. First, let's take another look at a couple of heroes to examine how they prepared for success and how their causes connected to their Life Wedge.

Learning from Leaders: The Jaime Escalante Story

Most often, when you encounter stories about heroes and recognized leaders, they are in a historical context. You might look at their impact on their cause or the world and how they have come to serve as a role model for others.

But I want you to see these heroes not just as historical figures but as real people, real examples of individuals living their values, supporting causes, and chasing dreams. I also want you to remember that in most cases, these individuals weren't born to fame; they were born to humble beginnings, just like you and me. The more we remember how much our heroes are really like us, the more we can learn from their stories, about where they came from, what they learned, the obstacles they overcame along the way, and how they prepared themselves for success.

Let's look now at a new example: Jaime Escalante, a high school math teacher at Garfield High School in East Los Angeles.

Jaime grew up in La Paz, Bolivia, the son of two teachers. He began teaching while still an undergraduate student in his home country, and in 1974, he was hired as a basic mathematics teacher at Garfield, a troubled inner-city school whose students, including gang members, were considered "unteachable" by many. But Jaime would not accept that idea or the idea that these students were any less smart or capable than any other students. He believed that as a teacher, he had the power to change the perception of the students and the students' perceptions of themselves. As he wrote in an article in 1990, "If motivated properly, any student can learn mathematics. Kids are not born as bad students; however, the school and the student's home and community environment can combine to produce a bad student. The teacher is the crucial point in this equation. It is up to the teacher to bring out the *ganas* [desire] in each student."[1] He also believes that math can be fun, that it can be taught with passion and humor, and that when students see this and realize that learning math can help them have a successful career, they can find the desire, focus, and discipline to learn.

From these beliefs grew Jaime's cause: the Advanced Placement program at Garfield High School. With this cause, Jaime committed himself to helping his students pass the Advanced Placement (AP) Calculus exam. He knew that by passing that exam, a student could receive college credit at more than 2,000 colleges and universities. But he also knew that "those who sit for the exam have already won the real game being played. They are winners because they have met a larger challenge than any single examination could present. They

---

[1]Quotes from Jaime Escalante are from an article that first appeared in the *Journal of Negro Education* 59, No. 3 (Summer 1990), published by the Bureau of Educational Research, Howard University, accessed at The Futures Channel Web site, www.thefutureschannel.com/jaime_escalante/jaime_escalante_math_program.php.

have attained a solid academic background in basic skills, especially math and science, and are prepared to move on and compete well against the challenges of both higher education and life."

His cause inspired action, in himself and others. First and foremost were hard work and the investment of time—he continually worked to prepare and improve his lessons, and he also committed himself to staying after school, every day, sometimes until 5:00 or 6:00 p.m., to help any student who needed extra assistance. When he showed how willing he was to put in the time, his students responded by investing their time and putting in the hard work as well.

Jaime also knew he needed help and that this effort required many resources. He enlisted the support of Ben Jimenez, a fellow math teacher at Garfield. He reached out to East Los Angeles College for help to offer summer school for his students when he could not teach it on the campus of the high school. He gained financial support from the ARCO Foundation and the National Science Foundation (NSF), which provided funds to help him expand the number of students, grade levels, and teachers in the summer program. He partnered with the Foundation for Advancements in Science and Education (FASE), which helped provide copiers, computers, transportation, and many other resources.

Soon, more and more of his students started taking the AP Calculus exam— and passing it. Jaime's efforts spread beyond math, as more students started taking more AP exams in more subjects. In 1978, the year before he started his AP program, only 10 AP tests were administered for the entire school, with none in calculus. Just 11 years later, in 1989, Garfield High School set a record with more than 450 AP tests administered, in 16 different subjects. In 1990, at a time when less than 2 percent of all high school seniors nationally took the exam, 25–30 percent of all Hispanics attempting the test nationwide originated from the Garfield program. Jaime's impact on Garfield went well beyond just AP exams. When he arrived there in 1974, there were only six Algebra I classes taught; 15 years later there were more than 25. Geometry and Algebra II classes grew from 10 to almost 30 in that same stretch.

The success of Jaime's program did not come without struggle. Many of his students challenged him in the early years, and many people doubted him along the way, including the Educational Testing Service (ETS), which administers the AP exams. In 1982, 18 of Jaime's students passed the AP Calculus exam, but ETS found the scores suspect, and asked 14 of the students who passed to take the exam again. Twelve agreed to take the test again (the other two decided they didn't need the credit for college), and all 12 scored well enough the second time to have their original scores reinstated.[2]

Jaime's story, including the saga with ETS, became the basis for the 1988 movie *Stand and Deliver*, featuring Edward James Olmos as Jaime. But even before the movie made him a hero to people across the world, his untiring commitment to his cause made him a hero to the students of Garfield High.

---

[2]Information regarding the Educational Testing Service challenge of exam scores was gathered from "Stand and Deliver Revisited," by Jerry Jessness, which originally appeared in July 2002, accessed from the online edition of *Reason* magazine, www.reason.com/news/show/28479.html.

Journal Entry: Escalante's Wedge

After reading Jaime Escalante's story, it's easy to identify his cause and his actions. But what about his values, his dream, and what went into his Life Wedge?

In your journal, reflect on Jaime's struggles and successes, and write down what you think his values, dreams, and goals were, and what you think he put into his Life Wedge. Then, write down how you think his cause, actions, and Life Wedge aligned to help him achieve success.

Finally, compare his Life Wedge to your Ideal Wedge: How are they similar? How are they different? What can you learn from Jaime's story and from thinking about how he achieved his success?

Analyzing the *Dream* Speech

We opened the chapter with the "I Have a Dream" speech, delivered by Martin Luther King Jr. Let's return to that speech, but let's look at it through a different lens: Think about Dr. King not as a historical figure but as a real person, as someone you might know. Specifically, I want you to think about Dr. King before he was a famous civil rights leader and instead imagine him as a college student at Morehouse College in Atlanta, Georgia, where he majored in sociology.

What made Martin Luther King Jr. the hero he became?

What do you think his life was like as a student? What sorts of classes do you think he took? What campus activities was he involved in? How did he spend his time outside of class? And how did all of those decisions, small and large, impact the man he became? How did his time at college forge his character and his career?

At the beginning of this chapter, you read a long excerpt from Dr. King's "I Have a Dream" speech. Revisit this excerpt, one paragraph at a time, and next to each paragraph, list the subjects he might have studied or the experiences he might have had as a college student that would have helped him to write and deliver this speech. Also, you might want to Google the entire speech and pull more examples from the rest of the text. What knowledge would he have needed to be able to make those statements? What courses might he have taken that would have helped him develop his thoughts on the specific topics? Next to the excerpt at the beginning of the chapter, draw an arrow connecting each of your notes (courses or experiences he may have studied) with a specific phrase or sentence of the speech.

Dr. King's Wedge

A WEDGE CHART OF DR. MARTIN LUTHER KING JR.'S LIFE

1. What was the goal of his life, that is, the cause for which he was willing to die?

2. As you look at the tasks and experiences you wrote nest to Dr. King's "I Have a Dream" speech, you can begin to understand

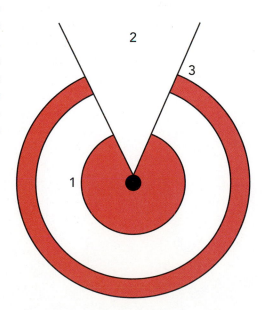

the areas to which he had committed time. These tasks and experiences enabled him, along with his passion for the cause itself, to give one of the most important speeches for the cause to and for which he gave his life. These tasks and experiences should be placed in the wedge. Based on other things you know about Dr. King's journey, what else could be placed in his wedge.

3. After filling his wedge, write things outside the wedge that could have easily distracted him. If you know about his life, perhaps there are things that he enjoyed but had to keep in perspective, that is, not giving the large chunks of time needed for the things in the wedge.

Journal Entry: Revisiting Your Wedge

In this chapter, we've taken a close look at heroes, their causes, and how those causes, along with the values, characteristics, and actions connected to them, contribute to their Life Wedges. As we wrap up, it's time to revisit *your* Life Wedge.

Each of us fills our Life Wedge with activities and commitments, sometimes by design and sometimes by default. Most of us commit to a cause or multiple causes the same way. It is my hope that as we progress through this book, you will realize the power you have to fill your Life Wedge and commit to a cause by design rather than by default and recognize that when you do choose to design your life and pursue worthy dreams, you have a much greater chance of success.

The Life Wedge principle is based on knowing where all of your energies are headed and understanding why. Now that you have thought about what the Life Wedges of several heroes might look like, take another look at yours.

In your journal, answer the following questions:

- How will your skills and strengths assist you in reaching your dream? What skills and strengths do you need to develop to help you get there? Are they currently in your Real Wedge? If not, how do you plan to put them there?

- In what ways do your values and ideals influence your Wedge commitments? What thoughts do you have about them after reading this chapter?

- Think for a few moments about one of your personal heroes as a college student. What do you think went into his or her Wedge? What knowledge, experiences, classes, and values helped him or her become your hero? How can you model your Wedge after your hero's Wedge?

Chapter 2 Review

SUMMARY OF MAJOR CONCEPTS

- A cause is an ideal or goal pursued with passion and dedication, bringing many people together to work toward shared goals.

- Noble causes have honorable qualities and are worthy of our energies; these causes fuel motivation and can help clarify life and career goals.

- Values are time-tested principles that help guide decisions and behavior and serve as the foundation for most causes.

- Heroes magnify commitment to noble causes, and their lives inform our own development. Often, our heroes' outstanding qualities are manifestations of their personal values.

- Alignment of causes, dreams, values, and actions increases the chance of success.

- Pursuit of noble causes often stems from intrinsic motivation, an internal drive resulting from a belief in something genuinely good in its nature.

- Regardless of why or how we entered college, we're more likely to be focused, disciplined, and excited about finishing if we become committed to a noble cause.

KEY TERMS

cause   an ideal or goal pursued with passion and dedication. In most cases, a cause brings many people together to work toward shared goals, and those efforts in turn affect many others.

values   time-tested principles that help guide decisions and behavior.

noble cause   a cause that is generally acknowledged to be founded on honorable values and qualities.

ignoble cause   a cause that is generally acknowledged to be founded on dishonorable values and qualities.

intrinsic motivation   an internal drive or reason behind actions and decisions that reflects genuine interest.

extrinsic motivation   a drive or reason behind actions and decisions that is inspired by external rewards or praise.

APPLICATION EXERCISE 1

Refining Goals

In Chapter 1, we began looking at goal setting. We looked at short-term goals and examined aspects of setting short-term goals that help keep us on track—deadlines, resources needed, possible obstacles, and "baby steps" to reach each goal. Take a moment now to review the short-term goals you set in the last chapter.

There exist as many approaches to setting goals as there are books on the subject, but in reviewing all the different strategies for goal setting, some common suggestions appear. The following goal-setting tips also can apply to your major life goals, but start by thinking about them in relation to your short-term goals.

Before we get to the list, keep two general principles in mind: "Manageable goals are measurable" and "Attainable goals have action steps." As you read through the following suggestions, you may want to go back to the goals you set in Chapter 1 and revise them.

1. **Be consistent with other goals.**

    Consider the pursuit of any goal in light of your other goals. For example, the goal to volunteer 10 hours a week at a local food pantry might work against your goal to improve your performance in a class if a study session meets at the same time the pantry needs volunteers. Considering goals in relation to other goals also forces you to evaluate your priorities and determine how well your goals and commitments fit into your Life Wedge.

2. **Focus on performance, not outcomes.**

    Goal setting appears to be more effective if your goal involves things that are more in your control than others' control. If you're an artist, a performance goal might be to paint a landscape of the caliber to be considered by studios. An outcome goal might focus on placing the painting in the Guggenheim Museum. The outcome goal is admirable, but realize that it is affected by many factors beyond your control, whereas you have full control over the performance goal.

3. **Be brief.**

    Long, rambling goals often include multiple goals or confuse the goal. Keep your goals simple and to the point.

4. **Be precise.**

    For example, instead of simply setting a goal "to paint a three-foot sea landscape," you might add, "that appeals to senior citizens in the San Diego area because of its tranquil beach." In addition to painting the landscape, the goal now adds the senior citizens, an ability to paint tranquility, and the ability to appeal to San Diego residents. The more precise your goal, the better you will be able to visualize accomplishing it.

5. **Be positive.**

    Don't establish defensive goals; rather focus on what you can do to improve your situation. There's nothing inspiring about a goal such as, "Don't fail

English class." Instead, focus on an aspect within the class and be positive about it, such as, "Be prepared for the first test in English."

6. **Be organized.**

   Record your goals in the same place each day. Computer programs make this simple, such as when you use the program Microsoft Outlook. Whether you keep a *Franklin Planner*, a notebook, or another form, write or type your goals so that you can keep tabs on them easily. Spending too much time on this part of the process can detract from actually reaching the goals.

7. **Be in control.**

   This might sound silly, but oftentimes we allow friends, relatives, and various others to determine our goals. They must be your goals if you want to pursue them whole-heartedly.

8. **Be well-informed.**

   Goals require information. You'll need to know the costs associated with your tasks, as well as the personal time and resources needed. Also, stay apprised of literature and updates that are germane to your interests, as this may help you achieve your goals.

9. **Be accountable.**

   Write down your goals with the expectation that you'll show them to someone else for input and for accountability. This could be a roommate, a staff member at the college, or a relative. You might find that you do well with your goals without much follow-up from others; however, if you continue to miss goals, ask others for help. You might want to offer to help someone else with his or her goals as well, for a fair exchange and to practice accountability.

APPLICATION EXERCISE 2

Tracking Your Second Week

In Chapter 1, you tracked the time you spent over a week. You're going to track your week again, but this time, you have a history to serve as a reference point. As you track your week with your actual time commitments, compare this week to your last week. What patterns do you notice? If there are changes between this week and the first week, what caused those? Were the changes simply the result of different things on your calendar, or did you make a conscious decision to operate differently? Either way, did your Life Wedge factor into how you spent your time?

Use Figure 2.1 (or whatever method you used in the last chapter, if you prefer) to track your time in half-hour segments. Again, be honest with your time tracking. Learning how you spend your time is a valuable tool for sharpening your Life Wedge.

FIGURE 2.1 Time Tracking Chart

Wedge Time-Tracking Sheet

Time of Day (M–F)	Monday	Tuesday	Wednesday	Thursday	Friday	List Two Main Time Commitments per Time Bloc	Time of Day (Weekend)	Saturday	Sunday	List Two Main Time Commitments per Time Bloc
7:00 AM to Lunch						1. _____ Amount of time: _____ 2. _____ Amount of time: _____	7:00 AM to Lunch			1. _____ Amount of time: _____ 2. _____ Amount of time: _____
Lunch to Supper						1. _____ Amount of time: _____ 2. _____ Amount of time: _____	Lunch to Supper			1. _____ Amount of time: _____ 2. _____ Amount of time: _____
Supper to 10:00 PM						1. _____ Amount of time: _____ 2. _____ Amount of time: _____	Supper to 10:00 PM			1. _____ Amount of time: _____ 2. _____ Amount of time: _____
10:00 PM to 3:00 AM						1. _____ Amount of time: _____ 2. _____ Amount of time: _____	10:00 PM to 3:00 AM			1. _____ Amount of time: _____ 2. _____ Amount of time: _____

At the end of the week, you'll be able to look at this chart and pick the items that are consuming most of your time. Since your weekends are likely much different than your weekdays, these are tracked separately. List the biggest consumers of your time within your Real Wedge—this is where you're actually spending your time. If you're having a difficult time listing anything of significance for a bloc of time, you might track your days literally by the hour. If you are not listing any concrete items, the implication is idle time (put "I"). Add your own abbreviations to simplify your tracking.

REMINDER

The Life Wedge exercises can be sketches on random papers and scraps throughout the week. You might find it helpful if losing attention in a class to doodle a wedge diagram and draw a connection from something in that course to a part of your ideal wedge.

3 The Connection to Class Work

When Am I Ever Going to Need This?

The first class I ever took as a college student was *Introduction to World Civilizations*, and by the end of the first lecture, I was ready to drop the course.

There was only one problem: I couldn't. The course was a general-education requirement, and I had to take it. Grudgingly, I went back for the second day, bracing myself to endure a full semester of material that held absolutely no interest for me. Then something funny happened during that second lecture: I was interested.

Instead of speaking in generalities, as he had done in the first lecture, the professor used historical examples that really grabbed my attention, mentioning big names like Napoleon, Alexander the Great, and the Reign of Terror. He also asked big questions: Why do some civilizations thrive, while others don't? Why have so many of the great civilizations enjoyed a glorious heyday, then collapsed? What decisions led to those collapses, and why have people throughout history made those decisions? What can we learn from these ancient civilizations that might be of value to us today?

I started not only paying attention but understanding that from the right perspective, history was much more than just names, dates, and battles—it was relevant and important to who we are today, and where we might be going.

As the semester progressed, *Introduction to World Civilizations* became my favorite class. I found myself thinking about these big questions of history on my own time, fascinated with the idea that there were pieces of evidence that helped unlock some of the mysteries in history itself, and I started looking at the course listings to see what other ancient history classes I could take.

Although I had arrived on campus with no grander purpose than following a few friends to college, I had found my passion: ancient history. And I had found it in a course I had desperately wanted to drop.

The Rigors and Requirements of the College Curriculum

I walked in to *Introduction to World Civilizations* unable to imagine how the content of the course could ever be relevant to my life—it was *ancient* history, after all—yet I walked out just a semester later having discovered my dream: to be an archaeologist and teach Greco-Roman history at the college level.

Would I have discovered my passion for the subject if I hadn't been required to take that class? It's possible but much less likely. And I'm hardly the only one to benefit from such a curriculum requirement—I've heard countless stories from students who discovered a major, a minor, a passion, or a life goal because of a required class they "had" to take.

But is that the reason for course requirements, to have you fall in love with a subject you previously knew nothing about?

Those happy accidents are great, but they're not the reasons schools establish curriculum requirements. (And don't think you're getting picked on; almost every school has curriculum requirements.) Requirements aren't there to frustrate you, waste your time, or give professors an excuse to ramble on about their favorite subject, either.

Institutions base their requirements on years of experience and the judgment of experts in the field of higher education. The objective of uniform requirements is to benefit not only students but also society by producing graduates with fundamental knowledge and competency. Many of the requirements are taking on more of a global context with the "Bologna Project." This is a movement within the European Union to streamline educational standards between countries (now including others outside the Union, such as China). And, in the light of books like Thomas L. Friedman's *The World Is Flat* (2005), we're reminded of the added pressure globally to take college seriously as our classrooms are actually not curved against the local students, but millions of students living in other countries that will be competing for the same future jobs.

You'll often hear that requirements will "help you to be a more well-rounded individual," and this is true as well. But what does that mean, and why does it matter? Being well-rounded means having basic knowledge in a wide range of subjects. This knowledge can enrich and complement your understanding of your primary interests by providing context, broadening your perspective, and helping you make connections between your primary interest and other subjects. It also can help you connect to and communicate with people who have different interests from you and help you understand cultural and historical references you will encounter in current events and the arts. (For instance, if your cultural literacy is limited to the things you've experienced firsthand, you're missing half the references on *The Simpsons*.)

Exploring other subjects also may inspire you to learn more about them. Many successful careers have been built because someone combined a primary interest with a secondary passion in an original, exciting way. Even if you don't pursue the subject as a major or as a career path, you may simply enjoy developing additional interests.

In summary, a broad base of knowledge helps you become an engaged participant in your culture and an informed citizen of the world. It also can open doors you might never have knocked on if you limited yourself to a single focus.

Eureka Moments Amidst the Requirements

I know what you're thinking: Being well-rounded sounds wonderful, but how does it help me survive a required class so far removed from my career interest that the only thing I can ever imagine applying the knowledge to is *Jeopardy!* questions?

In those situations, it can be a challenge to find the motivation to go to class, pay attention to the lecture, and invest energy in your assignments. I understand this, as do my fellow professors, and we do everything we can to make the material relevant and engaging to all our students, not just the ones majoring in it.

But you also have a responsibility to engage with the material, not just endure it. If your mindset is simply one of survival—*I'll do the minimum I can to get the lowest grade I can tolerate*—you'll miss out on eureka moments.

Eureka is an exclamation that translates from Greek as "I have found it!" According to legend, Hiero, king of Syracuse, commissioned a golden crown, but when the goldsmith returned with a crown equal in weight to the gold the king had given him, a charge was made that the crown was not pure gold and that (less valuable) silver had been mixed in with the gold.

Angry that he might have been duped, but not sure how to detect the trick, Hiero asked the mathematician Archimedes for help.

Archimedes was stumped until one day, while entering his bath, he noticed that the more he sank into the tub, the more water he displaced, which meant the displaced water was a measure of his volume. An idea struck: Because gold is heavier than silver, he could determine the purity of the crown by seeing how much water it displaced compared to gold of the same weight known to be pure.

Upon making this realization, the story goes, Archimedes leapt from the tub and ran naked through the streets of Syracuse, shouting, "Eureka! Eureka!" He had found a solution.

Today the word "eureka" indicates a discovery, especially an unexpected one, and a **eureka moment** has come to mean that instant when we find an answer someplace we never expected.

Eureka moments happen when we see, hear, read, or experience something that suddenly helps us understand a concept we've previously learned. They also occur when a nugget of knowledge stuck in the depths of our memory helps us solve a problem confronting us today.

The wonderful part of eureka moments is what pleasant surprises they are—you never know when they're going to happen. The frustrating part of eureka moments is . . . you never know when they're going to happen. But if you commit to being an engaged and active learner, no matter what class you're in, you'll plant seeds today that will blossom into eureka moments tomorrow.

In contrast, as the saying goes, if you snooze, you lose. And yes, we know when you sleep in class.

My Eureka Moments

What was your most recent eureka moment? Was it a moment when something suddenly made sense that hadn't made sense before? Did you see something unexpected that helped you solve a problem you'd been working on for days? Did something trigger a connection or application you hadn't previously considered?

Think for a moment about eureka moments you've experienced. These can be related to something you've learned in school or something nonacademic. In your journal, describe the eureka moment. Then write down what knowledge contributed to that moment, how you acquired that knowledge, and how it clicked for you in your eureka moment.

Connecting Class Work to Your Life Wedge

As we've discussed, you can't predict eureka moments; otherwise, they wouldn't be eureka moments.

Yet even without seeing into the future, you can examine a course you're taking now and understand how the material might prove helpful to you down the road.

To give a course or an assignment a fair analysis, start with your Ideal Wedge in mind. What have you placed there? What skills do you need to develop, what knowledge do you need to learn, and what experiences do you need to gain to help you realize your Ideal Wedge?

Your Ideal Wedge will suggest the *content* you need to succeed in your life pursuit. For example, if you've placed a career in engineering in your Life Wedge, you'll need to learn advanced math and physics. Those disciplines serve as the foundation for any engineering field.

Of course, if you're majoring in engineering, you're probably not wondering why you have to take all those math classes—the content is directly relevant. Instead, you're wondering why you have to take English classes, or history classes, or communication classes. You're wondering why you have to read the "classics," or, for that matter, any literature at all.

Conversely, if you're majoring in history, you might wonder why you have to take science classes. No matter your major, curriculum requirements oblige you to take some classes outside your chosen field.

When approaching these courses, ask yourself, "How can the knowledge I might learn in this class help with the *context* of my life pursuit?"

The context of nearly all careers involves **relationships**, **communication**, **perspective**, and **problem solving**. While some general education courses will help you with the content of your career interests—knowledge needed for specific tasks in your chosen field—they almost always help with the context.

If you're struggling to see how a course or an assignment will be relevant to you (beyond its required status), ask yourself the following questions to help you identify how what you're learning might fit in with the context of your life pursuit:

1. How can this help me **communicate** with my work colleagues?

2. How might this help me **communicate** my ideas with other audiences related to my job?

3. How might this help me establish and maintain positive work **relationships**?

4. How might this help me develop **relationships** among other audiences related to my job?

5. How does this help me gain **perspective** on information related to my career?

6. How does this assist me with **problem-solving** skills that might be helpful in my career?

Journal Entry: Finding Context

Think about a class you're taking right now that seems like "just a requirement" that you have to struggle through. (If you're not taking any class now that fits that description, think about a class you've taken in the past or an assignment that you didn't think was especially relevant to your life pursuit.)

With that class or assignment in mind, answer the six questions in the previous section about context.

After you've answered those questions, answer these additional questions:

• How has your perspective on that class or assignment changed since answering the context questions about it?

• How can these context questions help you the next time you are faced with a required course or assignment that doesn't initially sound interesting?

Reexamining Required Texts

It's always easier to see the relevance in things when you're looking back at them, but I want to give you a few examples of books that I was "required" to read as a college student that didn't seem applicable to me while I was reading them, but that I can now see were well worth my time.

Most of these books are still assigned at many colleges, and I hope you too have the opportunity to read and discuss them in a classroom environment.

Required Book: *Don Quixote,* Miguel de Cervantes (1605)

I understood that *Don Quixote* was a classic; I just didn't understand why I had to read it. The story in this Spanish novel follows a would-be knight, Don Quixote, fumbling along with his friend, Sancho Panza. In one scene, Quixote's misguided zeal clouds his reason as he boasts that God will help him slay "thirty or forty hulking giants." Panza realizes his friend is delusional and informs him that "Those over there are not giants but windmills." This episode gave rise to the idiom "tilting (jousting) at windmills," and the lesson is not just that Don Quixote is mad: Cervantes is challenging readers to expend energies on real needs in realistic ways. The term "quixotic" has come to mean striving for unrealistic ideals.

The content of *Don Quixote* seemed rather far from my major: My interest was in ancient history, not Spanish zealots. However, the book shed light on issues of context, helping me gain "perspective on information related to my career." The overall principle of not wasting time on unrealistic pursuits has helped me on many occasions. Like many classics, the book framed questions relevant to the characters as questions that spoke to the human condition. The book also helped me communicate with audiences, as most classics do, through demonstrating powerful writing.

Required Book: *Candide,* Voltaire (1759)

Candide, a poignant satire of the inconsistencies of many social, religious, and political groups, was required reading in a political science course. In the story, Candide finds himself expelled from the castle of a baron, who in turn loses all his possessions when the castle is ransacked. Throughout his varied and bizarre wanderings, Candide receives counsel from his former professor, Dr. Pangloss, who always focuses on the positive. Pangloss advises that regardless of how tragic and inhumane an episode Candide may suffer (and he suffers many), things are exactly how they are supposed to be, and we should accept them.

Voltaire challenges us to question such blind optimism. The story ends with Candide finally taking a practical approach to his life and ignoring Pangloss's unfounded ramblings. This book's witty insight into societal ills has helped me on many occasions to think through questions about ancient cultures. It definitely helps answer questions 5 and 6 about context (on perspective and problem-solving).

Required Book: *The Catcher in the Rye,* J.D. Salinger (1951)

The Catcher in the Rye was a stretch for me: I had a love–hate relationship with this controversial little book. So many people were raving about it, but I hated it. It felt like reading a Stephen King novel on your honeymoon—it was a dark, messy story that didn't fit my life. So I put it down, unfinished.

I picked it up again much later, after one of my students misrepresented it in his graduation speech, and decided it was time finally to finish it.

The key character in the story, 16-year-old Holden Caulfield, is actually in a psychiatric ward reflecting on the prior year (he's been expelled from his fourth different school). He finds hypocrisy everywhere, but in a mysterious way, in himself as well.

The book helps me with questions 2 and 4 above (about communication and relationships). On many occasions I've had bright students on the verge of academic failure—on dark, self-destructive searches. I've become more aware of their needs, and in cases when they weren't as clinically troubled as Holden, I was more sensitive and understanding in attempting to interest them in the course at hand. The book has served as a reference point in conversations with students and has helped me understand a few more.

Required Book: *The Structure of Scientific Revolutions,* Thomas Kuhn (1962)

The most difficult book of all the required texts I read was *The Structure of Scientific Revolutions*. Science was far afield from my major, not to mention my hunting and farming upbringing.

FIGURE 3.1   Book Chart

Name of book	Connect to content of my career	Connect to work colleauges	Connect to sharing ideas at work	Connect to maintain work relationships	Connect to developing relationships	Connect to gaining perspective	Connect to problem-solving
Eureka experience: Book:			Discovery connected to your future:				

Although the book bored me to tears with a barrage of examples from science, I stuck with it and found several valuable insights. Besides learning that farming is based on science, I also discovered that the book's main thesis about paradigm (worldview) shifts applies to any historical time, ancient or present. When paradigm shifts happen with new discoveries, many people resist them and try to prop up the old ways of seeing things. This book spoke to both the content and context of my career path, assisting with many of the context questions, especially number 6 (problem-solving). Being cognizant of changing worldviews among audiences has helped me communicate clearly on many fronts.

In time I began to understand more fully the purpose of the curriculum and that these required courses and their books were intentionally placed on my path. I know today that I'm a much better traveler for having stopped to engage them, and I can see how these classes and texts offered lessons that have transcended time and career choices.

Every book in each of your classes has been intentionally placed on your college path as well. In the chart in Figure 3.1, select five required books you have read, or are currently reading, and identify how they connect to the content of your anticipated career, as well as the six context questions from the previous section. Then explain a eureka moment you've had with one of the books.

Learning from Logic and Reasoning

We can also use logic to help us understand the purpose of our academic efforts. When we find ourselves saying, "This makes no sense" or "What difference does this make?" we are begging for the use of logic to lead us to a deeper understanding.

The basic forms of logic are usually categorized as *deductive* and *inductive*.

Deductive logic (or deductive reasoning) is the process of determining a specific conclusion based on general knowledge. In other words, deductive logic uses the big picture—universal laws or principles—to make sense of the small picture.

With deductive reasoning, we attempt to make sense of a situation by starting with some key concepts or truths. Consider what happens when another student approaches you to join her political cause. Maybe you don't have all the particulars about the issues the group supports, but you know some of the general ideals espoused by that particular group. In such a case, you can "deduce" whether to join. This is deductive reasoning.

The Basic Deductive Argument Structure: Syllogisms

While many other rules govern deductive logic, the three-line argument or logic forms called ***syllogisms*** serve as the basic deductive argument structure. In these arguments, the conclusion stems directly from two main facts (or premises). The structure looks like this:

Premise 1: _____

Premise 2: _____

Conclusion: _____

For example:

Premise 1: College graduates are more likely to have higher-paying jobs than nongraduates.

Premise 2: My friend is a college graduate.

Conclusion: Therefore, my friend is more likely to have a higher-paying job than a nongraduate.

In a deductive argument, if the premises are both true and there is commonality between them, the conclusion will be true. You'll notice that in both of the above premises, the common element is college graduation. In the following syllogism, the common element is location.

Premise 1: The University of Notre Dame is west of Boston College.

Premise 2: Gonzaga University is west of the University of Notre Dame.

Conclusion: Therefore, Gonzaga University is west of Boston College.

Be warned though: If the premises are false, or they are not in common, then the conclusion is not guaranteed (or *valid*). For example:

Premise 1: All college presidents are unaware of YouTube (false premise).

Premise 2: She is a college president (true premise).

Conclusion: Therefore, she is unaware of YouTube (invalid conclusion because of false premise).

In this case, the deductive argument breaks down immediately because the first premise is not true—many presidents are tech-savvy. And with a syllogism, if only one college president is aware of YouTube, this argument doesn't guarantee the conclusion.

The next example falls apart not only because of potentially false premises, but also because it lacks commonality (also referred to as *inference* or *entailment*):

> Premise 1: All students dislike cafeteria food (possibly false premise).
>
> Premise 2: All administrators dislike cafeteria food (possibly false premise).
>
> Conclusion: Therefore, all administrators are students (invalid conclusion because of false premise and lack of commonality—there is no established membership that is identical between students and administrators).

The more informed you are, and the more exposure you have to different perspectives, the more you will be able to assert true premises and make valid connections, which will help ensure that your logic is sound. Courses, textbooks, internships, mentoring relationships, and informational interviews with people in your area of interest will help you get a better understanding of the knowledge you will need in your chosen field, and this understanding will help you connect your current course work to your future career.

Journal Entry: Applying Deductive Logic to Your Course Work

Think of a particular course whose value and relevance you've been questioning and at least two assignments in particular for which you've struggled to find a connection.

In your journal, draft a syllogism for each assignment that helps remind you of the reason behind it. If possible, your syllogism should help you connect the assignment with a long-term goal. For example, if you have an interest in assisting with a community program but find yourself struggling to maintain interest in math class, you might quickly outline the following:

> Premise 1: Budgets are needed to run community organizations.
>
> Premise 2: Basic math is needed to keep budgets.
>
> Conclusion: Therefore, basic math is needed to run a community organization.

Once you've completed these syllogisms, you might want to pin them to your bulletin board to remind you about the value of your coursework. This exercise can be helpful whenever you're feeling frustrated with a course or an assignment.

Inductive Reasoning

Whereas syllogisms may at times seem too abstract, ***inductive reasoning*** often feels more closely linked to common sense. When you use inductive reasoning, you take the opposite approach from deductive reasoning: You begin with the small and work to the large. As you move from the specific to the general, you examine individual instances or pieces of information and identify their connections and common truths to draw a conclusion.

Scientists used this approach when determining the law of gravity—they observed the characteristics of matter and planetary movements, then came to a conclusion or general observation (a rule or law).

A scenario closer to your experience might be noticing a series of poor test scores in a particular class, a difficulty learning certain subject matter, and other negative feedback that might cause you to reconsider your choice of major.

You also can find plenty of examples of inductive reasoning on TV. Think about crime dramas such as *CSI*, *Cold Case*, and *Bones* or, in the case of *House*, a medical drama. Each episode starts with the big picture—a murder victim or a mysteriously sick patient—and then investigators or doctors try to solve the crime or crisis using a series of small clues. As they accumulate clues, they develop general theories, which they then test and retest as they gather more clues, until the mystery is solved.

The inductive approach is extremely helpful in unpacking the relevance of our schedules. We can envision the big picture—the goal in our Life Wedge, or a career path. Using inductive reasoning, we can think like an investigator and identify whether the individual clues—classes, activities, internships, readings—will help us lead to the solution we're looking for, our life goal. Inductive reasoning can help not only make sense of your daily choices but also with the actual processing of information in classes.

The Basic Inductive Argument Structures

Although there are many types of inductive arguments, they all rely on collecting pieces of information. In a sense, inductive reasoning is about being observant as you progress through college—paying attention to the experiences, the pieces of information, and the clues that you will find on your path. Consider the following observation:

> I have noticed many students that skip classes don't submit homework. They must not care about their grades.

This example contains three observations:

- There are many students involved in the observation.

- This group has attendance problems and shirks responsibility.

- There could be a reason the students are acting this way (maybe all are related and have had deaths in their family, or perhaps they're athletes on the same team and have excused absences for tournaments).

While the third observation could be true, common sense leads us to believe that students who skip class and don't submit homework will likely fail or receive poor grades. Inductive logic, however, provides a more analytical approach than common sense to help us think systematically and determine the validity of our thoughts.

Consider the following as one way to outline inductive logic: Many students claim that since there is no attendance policy in certain classes, they can manage just fine without going to class. Perhaps this is true, on occasion, and maybe it's true for certain individuals. But is it generally true? Is it a wise practice? The following is a way to frame the logic. Each "Instance" is a person, "A" refers to the number of classes missed, and "X" is the consequences:

Instance 1 of A = X	I saw Juan skip 20 classes; he received a grade reduction.
Instance 2 of A = X	Mary told me she skipped 20 classes; she received a "D."
Instance 3 of A = X	Sally sits in front of me, and she missed 20 classes and earned an "F."
Instance 4 of A = X	Alberto missed 20 classes and got an "F."
Instance 5 of A = X	Liska missed 20 classes and had to retake the class.
Instance 6 of A = X	Padmathia skipped 20 classes and failed.

Therefore, instance 7 of A will likely equal X.

Instance 7	Jordon just missed his 20th class and therefore will likely receive a poor grade.

And therefore, all A = X.

This is a "general" finding that all students skipping an excessive number of classes—in this case, 20—will get lower grades. It is based on the "particular" instances of 1–6. This is a *universal generalization* form of inductive reasoning; that is, each of the people had something in common and experienced common results.

Whether examining a situation with a deductive or an inductive argument, applying this process is a proactive way to identify logical connections between different aspects of our lives. Although people often think of logic exercises as only applicable in a philosophy class, the reality is that the logic and ways of thinking we learn in philosophy class help us understand our own life situations.

Journal Entry: Applying Inductive Logic to Your College Life

Imagine a detective has been assigned to a mysterious case: your college career.

In your journal, write down the pieces of "evidence" the detective might find while investigating you. What "clues" would provide critical information about who you are, what you're interested in, how you conduct yourself, and what life goals you might be pursuing? What would these pieces of information reveal? As the detective steps back to look at all of the evidence, what big picture could be seen?

When you conclude your detective work, consider these questions: Do the specific instances and examples in your daily life lead you to the big-picture conclusion you've defined for yourself in your ideal Life Wedge? If so, how? If not, what changes might you consider?

Choices: Defining Our Path to, through, and beyond College

We've spent most of this chapter talking about courses you're required to take, assignments you're required to complete, and books you're required to read. But while many requirements are placed before you, your college experience will ultimately be defined by the choices you make.

You will choose a major (or two) and perhaps a minor (or three); you will choose electives within your disciplines and electives that just sound cool; you will choose extracurricular activities and social activities; you will choose which campus speakers to attend and which to skip; you will choose your friends and your roommates, your professors and your study partners.

All these choices and the many more you will make in the next few years will define your path through college. Much as your path *to* college serves as a foundation for your path *through* college, your path *through* college will serve as a foundation for your path *beyond* college. That's why I don't recommend wandering randomly or aimlessly down your college path.

If you've taken our discussions in this and previous chapters about goals, dreams, and life pursuits seriously, you should be getting comfortable avoiding the "aimlessly" part. But even with a plan, you'll face decisions every day that don't connect directly to your Life Wedge, where there is no clear "right" choice. What then?

In "The Road Not Taken," the poet Robert Frost tells of encountering a choice of paths to take:

> Two roads diverged in a yellow wood,
> And sorry I could not travel both
> And be one traveler, long I stood
> And looked down one as far as I could
> To where it bent in the undergrowth;
>
> Then took the other, as just as fair,
> And having perhaps the better claim,
> Because it was grassy and wanted wear;
> Though as for that the passing there
> Had worn them really about the same,
>
> And both that morning equally lay
> In leaves no step had trodden black.
> Oh, I kept the first for another day!

Yet knowing how way leads on to way,
I doubted if I should ever come back.

I shall be telling this with a sigh
Somewhere ages and ages hence:
Two roads diverged in a wood, and I—
I took the one less traveled by,
And that has made all the difference.[1]

The narrator is a traveler presented with two tempting choices. Both look ripe with opportunity and potential, but the narrator chooses the one less traveled, knowing both that he can save the path more traveled for another day and that he's not likely to pass that way again. If he could travel both, he would, but he is only one traveler. He must choose.

As a college student, you are faced with similar choices. Often, taking one class means not taking another that also interests you because both are offered at the same time. Choosing one major may mean not choosing a different one that also appeals to you because completing the requirements for both would be too demanding.

Even where you go to school represents a similar choice that you've already made. If you are at a large public school, you chose not to attend a small private college. If you enrolled at a traditional rural campus, you chose not to take classes at an urban community college. Undoubtedly, you're missing out on things you might have enjoyed had you chosen a different college experience, but we are each only one person, so we must choose.

Being Observant on the Road Taken

Once our choices are made though, our job as traveler calls for more than just plowing ahead. The wise traveler is also observant on the road taken.

Fundamentally, being an observant traveler means paying attention and giving appropriate thought and reflection to the bends in the path and the options we encounter. I believe that to be truly observant also means looking back at our decisions, to assess them and the impact they have made on our current path.

One way to improve our observation skills is to record our thoughts, as you have been doing with the journaling exercises in this book. However, I encourage you to make thoughtful reflection a regular part of your life, beyond the structured activities in this course. The journaling questions we have used can serve as an effective starting point for your own journaling, as can our discussion in the previous section about deductive and inductive logic. As you observe your choices on your path to and through college, what does inductive

---

[1]Robert Frost, "The Road Not Taken," *The Poetry of Robert Frost,* Edward Connery Lathem, ed. Copyright © 1916, renewed 1944 by Robert Frost.

reasoning suggest about where your path might be headed? Looking at the road taken, what can you deduce about individual decisions you have made?

Your goal in journaling and reflective thought is to understand better the path you have chosen and ultimately to understand yourself better. Which choices turned out as you hoped? Why? Which choices did not turn out as you hoped? Why? What have you learned about yourself and your decision-making process? How can this knowledge help you make wiser decisions in the future?

Ultimately, everything that crosses our path helps define our journey; whether or not these encounters prove enriching is usually up to us. Observation and reflection not only help us put our experiences in context, but they help us mature and grow.

We will never stop encountering choices along our path, in college or beyond. The more observant we are about where our path has led and how we've traveled it, the more prepared we will be to make smart choices about where we're going.

Journal Entry: Observations on Your College Path

Take a few moments to reflect on your path through college thus far. Even if you're just a few weeks into your first term as a college student, you've already made dozens of choices that have impacted, in ways large and small, where you are today.

In your journal, identify three choices you have made since you've been at college. These choices can be about classes, activities, or how and where you've studied. After writing down each of these choices, answer the following questions about each choice:

- Why did you make this choice? How much thought did you give the choice? What criteria did you consider before making the choice?

- If you had this choice to make over again, would you make the same choice? Why or why not?

- What have you learned from this choice that will help you make better choices in the future?

Rosa Parks and the Crossroads Principle

No matter what road you travel, you're bound to encounter intersections.

On December 1, 1955, Rosa Parks decided she would take a stand—or a seat, as it were. The story is now familiar: When the unknown seamstress from Montgomery, Alabama, refused to give up her seat on the bus to a white passenger, the bus driver had her arrested. By many counts, the modern civil rights movement had begun.

Many people think her action was spontaneous. However, her decision to break a local ordinance was not her first public action committed to the cause of racial equality. She had been advocating justice and dignity for years in her community.

"I worked on numerous cases with the NAACP, but we did not get the publicity. There were cases of flogging, peonage, murder, and rape," she said in an interview years after the famous incident. "We didn't seem to have too many successes. It was more a matter of trying to challenge the powers that be, and to let it be known that we did not wish to continue being second-class citizens."[2]

For Parks, the situation on the bus represented a significant intersection. She had come to a crossroads. She could quietly move to the back of the bus, continuing to allow herself to be defined as a second-class citizen, or she could refuse.

In that moment, all her work for justice and all her learning about equality crystallized in a life situation that tested her abstract beliefs. Her answer to the test—the choice she made at that personal crossroads—changed history. When asked why she refused to move to the back of the bus, she replied, "Because I was tired." She wasn't only tired from a long day of hard work. She was tired of injustice.

The ***Crossroads Principle*** is about the choices we make when we come to the major intersections along our path.

When we come to a crossroads, our formal learning and our informal experiences intersect, helping us make informed choices and internalize what we've learned. When we encounter a crossroads between our academic path and a life situation, we can put our book knowledge into a real-world context.

For example, we might learn the formula for right angles in geometry but only understand its value when helping to square a foundation for a Habitat for Humanity home. We might enjoy learning about personality profiles but feel they're abstract until we encounter our first boss, who exhibits a "Type A" personality. Perhaps an English Composition class will feel tedious and detached from our desire to be a nurse until we begin writing letters to help raise funds for installing defibrillators in our local schools.

These instances of the Crossroads Principle can happen when something you've learned from one class intersects with a problem in another, but quite often, you'll find a crossroads situation outside the classroom.

Educators call this ***experiential learning*** because you are not learning just from texts and lectures but from a firsthand experience. If this learning involves an act of helping another person or assisting a cause, it's called ***service learning***.

Experiential learning and service learning often occur unexpectedly, but they also can be placed on our path, either by professors (such as a cross-cultural dialogue or field trip) or by us through our decisions. As we discussed in the last section, these crossroads experiences, and indeed every learning experience, can be enhanced by reflecting on the path we have traveled.

---

[2]American Academy of Achievement, "Rosa Parks: Pioneer of Civil Rights," Interview June 2, 1995, Williamsburg, Virginia, www.achievement.org/autodoc/page/par0pro-1 (accessed October 21, 1997).

Journal Entry: Lessons from the Crossroads

Think of a situation when you have experienced the Crossroads Principle. This could be something significant, when you were challenged to put your ideals into action, as Rosa Parks was on that bus in Montgomery, or simply a time when knowledge gained in the classroom intersected with a life experience in a way that enhanced your learning.

In your journal, explain your crossroads experience and what you learned from it.

The Story of "The Crossroads"

My family lives in Weaver, Indiana, originally called "The Crossroads." It was a historic black community built around two intersecting roads, and it once included hundreds of families, two schools, a racetrack, two churches, and numerous "black farms." Weaver came into existence for one reason—blacks were not welcome in the nearby cities. Through the gains of civil rights advocates, sensible legislation was eventually passed, and the black families from Weaver began moving into the cities of Marion and Indianapolis.[3]

Although the civil rights gains in Weaver's nearby cities occurred long before Rosa Parks's act of courage and her message about justice and equality, it still resounded with the Weaver emigrants, who were all too familiar with the ugliness of racism. In 1930, the last lynching in America took place in Marion, a few miles north of Weaver.[4]

That message resonates with my African-American neighbors today. Our area of Grant County has made great strides in addressing these issues, recently electing the state's first African-American sheriff, Oatis Archey.

The values Rosa Parks stood for helped end the need for towns like Weaver. Weaver, built in an out-of-the-way place, ceased to exist as a functioning town around 1900 and officially closed in 1929. All that remains today are four scattered houses, including the farm where my family lives. The rest of the buildings are gone, except for the African Methodist Episcopal (A.M.E.) church—and one billboard.

Every time we drive down our road, 600 South, we cross 300 West, where this lone billboard marks the legacy of Weaver. Each time we pass this billboard, my family and I experience something of a crossroads moment because the story of "The Crossroads" in Indiana and its theme that runs through the entire civil rights movement intersects directly with our lives every day.

When we pass that billboard and my sons are in the car with me, I often reflect on the world they are inheriting, on how much more enlightened their generation will be than ones before them, and yet how much the issues that necessitated "The Crossroads" must not be forgotten.

---

[3]Matthew T. Voss and Aaron P. Sickler, "Life at the Crossroads," Video (Marion, IN: Marion Public Library, 1998); Rolland Lewis Whitson, *Centennial History of Grant County 1812–1912,* 2 vols. (Chicago: The Lewis Publishing Co., 1914), pp. 348–57, 1384–86.

[4]Alistair Cooke, *Alistair Cooke's America* (New York: Alfred A. Knopf, 1973), pp. 311–12.

My boys know Rosa Parks's story, and they've been challenged to reflect on the need and reasons for her actions. They understand that her stand for dignity on that bus ride in 1955 helps identify the indignity of racism today. And every day, they travel a road that literally intersects with black history. Whether they're with their African-American cousins or just driving past that billboard, they appreciate the various diversity issues that impact their lives and the values behind them. Because of their frequent exposure to the Crossroads Principle, they have taken ownership of those values and those issues; they're not just abstract concepts or pieces of history. As often as possible, I challenge my boys to think about the actions they will choose and the decisions they will make when they come to their own crossroads.[5]

Journal Entry: A Landmark Crossroads on Your Path

Odds are, as you travel to and from school each day, you pass a number of landmarks that commemorate significant crossroads in history. Perhaps it's a statue of someone who stood for a cause, a street or a bridge named after someone who made a difference, or a plaque that recognizes an important accomplishment.

Think about the path you travel each day and what landmarks you pass. Pick one, and the next time you pass it, take a closer look. Pause to think about what crossroads that landmark represents. In your journal, record a few reflections about that landmark and what thoughts came to mind when you stopped to consider it as an example of the Crossroads Principle.

---

[5]For the author's newsprint article on the *Crossroads Principle,* see www.indwes.edu/buckcreek, and click on "Afro at the Crossroads."

Chapter 3 Review

SUMMARY OF MAJOR CONCEPTS

- College courses usually help with both the content and context of our life pursuits. General education courses more often help with the context.

- The context of nearly all jobs involves relationships, communication, perspective, and problem solving—where connections to course work are often made.

- Sound logic, such as deductive or inductive reasoning, enables us to make more sense of life experiences and their connection to our college commitments.

- The Crossroads Principle is when formal and informal learning intersect, and we are more likely to internalize the meaning of the new knowledge.

KEY TERMS

eureka moment   derived from the Greek word "eureka," which translates as "I have found it!" today the word "eureka" indicates a discovery, especially an unexpected one, and a "eureka moment" has come to mean that instant when we find an answer someplace we never expected.

deductive logic   the process of determining a specific conclusion based on general knowledge.

syllogism   a three-line argument or logic form that serves as the basic deductive argument structure. In these arguments, the conclusion stems directly from two main facts (or premises).

inductive reasoning   the process of making a generalization based on specific knowledge.

Crossroads Principle   the principle that describes what happens when our formal learning and our informal experiences intersect, helping us make informed choices and internalize what we've learned.

experiential learning   learning gained from first-hand experience rather than from texts and lectures.

service learning   a type of experiential learning that involves helping another person or assisting a cause.

APPLICATION EXERCISE

Recognizing Learning Preferences

Throughout this book, we've looked at the big picture, then tried to make sense of it. We began with the Life Wedge, identifying first a main goal or life cause, and then looking at the pieces that help get us there. This approach plays to the right side of your brain, the side that processes information creatively and holistically. Some people are "right-brain dominant" because they prefer to learn this way—they are visual learners. They look at the context first, such as a sentence or general story, instead of a single word or event. This is important stuff according to the Nobel Prize committee: It awarded its coveted honor to the founder of this theory of bi-hemispheric processing, Roger W. Sperry, in 1981.

In our discussion of logic, we considered processes that tend to be more easily processed by those who are "left-brain dominant." That is, they look at logical or sequential patterns. They think linearly, from point "A" to point "P." It appears that the majority of classroom assignments favor this type of processing.

Various quizzes can be found on the Web to test your preferences, such as "The Hemispheric Dominance Inventory Test," by Intelegen Inc., at http://brain.web-us.com/brain/braindominance.htm. Also see Similarminds .com and Chatterbean.com.

You might want to go online and take one of these tests, though they vary widely in quality. However, for now, look at the list of majors and attributes that tend to align with what many scholars claim are right- and left-brain dominance. Usually, students seem to identify which side aligns more closely with their preferences. It's key to remember that neither side has the advantage over the other or is "better." Both work together but process information differently. As you look at the following chart, identify whether you identify yourself primarily with right- or left-brain dominance. Also, add a few attributes under each and possible majors that align with these attributes.

Right Brain Dominance		Left Brain Dominance	
Common College Majors	Attributes	Attributes	Common College Majors
History	Visual	Verbal	Math
Literature	Simultaneous	Sequential	Philology (study of languages)
	Intuitive	Analytical	Science
	Random processing	Linear processing	Writing
	Finds similarities	Finds differences	Logic
	Subjective	Objective	

Various educators note that colleges and K–12 schools need to improve their efforts at targeting curriculum for "whole-brain" development, not overlooking right-brain processing. The helpful *Funderstanding* site (http://www .funderstanding.com/right_left_brain.cfm), produced by On Purpose Associates, argues that this could happen "by incorporating more patterning, metaphors, analogies, role playing, visuals, and movement into their reading, calculation, and analytical activities." As you look at your current assignments, can you identify any of the above activities? List a couple of these below and comment on how you find them helpful, or a distraction:

1. _____

   _____

2. _____

   _____

The major advantage of recognizing your learning preferences is to capitalize on them and utilize exercises that work for you regardless of the subject. If you're a visual learner, keep that in mind while studying abstract philosophical concepts. Find a way to diagram or picture your subjects. If you're a logical or sequential learner, use steps or charts to categorize things you find overly creative or elusive.

A sign of maturing as a student and learner is being observant. Identifying your learning preferences is a key step in this direction.

REMINDER

In the previous two chapters, you kept time charts to inform your Life Wedge chart. Have you transferred the basic time chunks onto your "real" Life Wedge?

2 The Big Picture Approach

Driving toward the Big Picture.

Shoot for the Right Goals*

As I swished my long-distance jump shot, the packed gym roared.

Suddenly I was very alone. They were the wrong fans and that was the wrong basket.

In the celebrated Indiana state basketball tournament, I had earned legendary status in an instant, and for all the wrong reasons. My team lost. I retired as a freshman.

Throughout my Buck Creek youth, I pretended to hit the winning shot. I reenacted Rick Mount's fade-away buzzer-beater from the corner against Marquette. I pretended to dribble like Billy Keller, to glide like Oscar Robertson, to spin like Pistol Pete.

And there, in a real-live game situation, I hit the long jumper at the buzzer, just as I had done all those days in my mind, and I experienced the applause. For a few brief, euphoric moments, I was living a dream.

With a few seconds left, the coach inserted two new players. They immediately ran to the wrong basket and yelled, "We're open!" As the shooting guard, I shot. The only consolation, in retrospect, is that there was no three-point line.

The throbbing noise of laughing foreign fans somehow became muted. An out-of-body experience ensued. I wanted to pull my knee-high gold-striped tube socks over my shaggy head and disappear. All three of us—the majority of our team—had run to the wrong end. I had taken the shot.

I've relived the nightmare for a lifetime since, starting with the consolation game the next night, in which the clever opposing fans shouted, "Shoot!" every time I pulled down a defensive rebound.

Needless to say, it's pretty disheartening to discover you've shot at the wrong goal.

While speaking at various national educational conferences during my post-basketball career, I've discovered many well-meaning educators who are also shooting at the wrong basket.

In an effort to help students succeed—to graduate—many college programs have become focused not on motivating students toward success but on moving them through the system.

I surveyed educators from more than 400 institutions and discovered that many of their programs focus on addressing areas of student dissatisfaction. These colleges survey students and determine what is most important to them and in what areas they're most satisfied or dissatisfied.

It's both helpful and necessary to have a pulse on student perceptions. The theory behind these surveys seems logical: Determine what students deem as most important, ascertain which of those areas are the most dissatisfying, and then address those areas in an effort to "retain" students. In other words, students are like customers, and happy customers are more likely to stay until they graduate.

Of course, once you realize the flaws in seeing students as customers, you understand how this approach can address student dissatisfaction without actually helping students succeed.

Fredrick Herzberg's research shows that removing dissatisfaction does not mean that one is satisfied and that areas of dissatisfaction actually have little to do with true motivation.

The movie *Stand and Deliver*, based on a true story, is an excellent illustration of the motivation-driven model for student success. In the film, high-school math teacher Jaime Escalante helps his students in a poor East Los Angeles neighborhood—Hispanic students regularly written off by other educators—excel despite endless dissatisfactions in an abysmal educational situation. They committed to a cause (passing the AP Calculus exam and going to college) and were motivated to succeed. He addressed what educators call the student core.

In other words, while the majority of his colleagues screamed from the other end of the court, he shot at the right basket, proving that all students are capable of learning and can be motivated by goals, noble causes, and their underpinning values.

When you're watching the game from the perspective of the bleachers, it's easy to spot when a disoriented freshman is aiming at the wrong net. But standing on the court with the ball in your hands and the clock ticking down, it's easy to get flustered and confused by the decisions you face.

While having dinner at the Escalantes' Pasadena home, I was reminded of Jaime's success at student success—even though he set out to teach math. Award plaques were stacked like dominos in the garage, and some in a hallway, while only a few awards were actually on display. Jaime didn't see much of a need to mount his achievements on the wall because he understood that it wasn't about him, and it certainly wasn't about awards—rather, it was about his students and helping them pursue the right goals.

The majority of Escalante's colleagues yelled for him to get with the program and do things the way they did, but he stayed focused on a different goal—true student success, rather than mere student nondissatisfaction.

AUTHOR'S COMMENTS

The very fact that you're reading this book reflects a belief among your professors and staff that motivation is important. We all need assistance in many ways, and it's important to deal with any areas of dissatisfaction—but not as important as the decision to focus on your core beliefs and to connect them with life goals.

QUESTIONS

1. Have you ever worked hard for something, only to realize that you were shooting for the wrong goal?

2. Have you had a professor or teacher like Jamie Escalante who motivated you? If so, what was it about him or her that connected with you?

3. What do you think are the most important aspects of your college experience related to your future—to your life passion or career?

4. If you could step out of the college experience for a few minutes and sit in the bleachers and observe, what would you perceive as the key goals of your university for your education?

5. An increasing number of colleges are focusing on "the student core." This next chapter will examine areas related to this core, especially dispositions—the role of your beliefs. You will learn how to frame an approach to understand your personal connection to your college's mission. What personal goals resonate with your college experience—goals that are at the right end of the court?

* Jerry Pattengale, "Shoot for the Right Goals," *Chronicle Tribune* (Paxton Media) April 17, 2003.

4 Willpower and Waypower

The Forging of a Nation

Things looked bleak for George Washington's troops, and not just because the frigid Pennsylvania winter showed no signs of relenting. Just three months earlier, on September 11, British forces had conquered Philadelphia in the Battle of Brandywine. Congress had fled the capitol, heading west to York for safety. When Washington's army marched into camp at Valley Forge on December 19, 1777, they were cold, tired, and ill-equipped. Many of the men lacked blankets to lie upon; others had no shoes to protect their feet. Some were without clothes, exposed to the elements, and countless soldiers suffered through long nights outside until shelters could be built to shield them.

Making matters worse, as they decamped to Valley Forge on the heels of two key defeats, General Washington's army lacked much of the training needed for consistent success on the battlefield against the professional soldiers of the British Army.[1]

And yet, just six months later, on June 19, 1778, this same army emerged to pursue and successfully engage Lt. Gen. Sir Henry Clinton's British army at the Battle of Monmouth, in New Jersey. They demonstrated the military precision of ordered ranks, which combined with their revived spirit and tremendous fighting skill to lead them to victory. Amidst the cold, sickness, and hardship that defined that long winter in Valley Forge, a transformation had taken place—a transformation that turned the course of the war, and of history.

How did this happen? While historians will point to strategy, tactics, and leadership, at its core, the story of Washington's army at Valley Forge is one of **willpower** and **waypower**.

Washington's route to Valley Forge

---

[1]Source: Valley Forge Historical Society.

A Powerful Resolve

"To see men without clothes to cover their nakedness," Washington wrote on April 21, 1778, "without blankets to lie upon, without shoes . . . without a house or hut to cover them until those could be built, and submitting without a murmur, is a proof of patience and obedience which, in my opinion, can scarcely be paralleled."

The patience and obedience to which Washington referred owed directly to the soldiers' sense of purpose. While conditions were unquestionably challenging, and there were deserters throughout that long winter, the soldiers generally maintained a positive outlook, dutifully building a camp, training, and looking forward to spring, when they would have the opportunity to fight the British once again. What drove them? The willpower that came from their pursuit of a noble cause. These men were fighting for their freedom. They knew that if they lost this war, their new homeland would lose its independence.

One of the many reasons Washington is known as a great military leader is that his will and sense of belief in what his army was there to do set the tone for his soldiers. As the description that accompanies Charles Wilson Peale's 1780 portrait of the general at Valley Forge National Historical Park explains, "From the day he took command of the Continental Army in 1775, Gen. George Washington's faith in the moral rightness of the American cause never wavered. The character and purpose that helped sustain him and his soldiers at Valley Forge is reflected in [this] portrait of the general."[2]

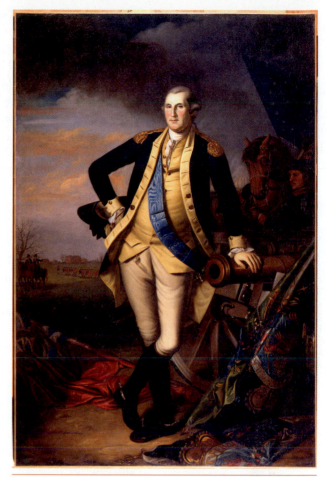

Charles Wilson Peale's 1780 portrait of General Washington, which hangs at Valley Forge National Historical Park.

Help on the Way

Willpower was essential for surviving the harsh winter and preparing to mount another campaign, but it was bolstered by waypower.

Brutal as it was, the winter weather actually provided a reprieve for the Continental Army. Cold, snowy conditions limited transportation for both sides and kept them from attempting any maneuvers, giving Washington's troops the opportunity to regroup. Although supplies were scarce when they first arrived, the soldiers quickly set about turning Valley Forge into a proper camp. They located supplies in the area and built log cabins for shelter.

---

[2]Ibid.

Under the direction of military engineers, some 2,000 huts were built, miles of trenches were dug, and a bridge was constructed over the Schuylkill River. Surgeons and nurses came to help fight off disease and restore sick and wounded soldiers to health. Many women followed the army to Valley Forge and helped with such vital services as sewing, laundering, and nursing. With each passing week, with each new hut, with each new trench, the army's confidence grew. They applied their will to finding ways, big and small, to become a stronger, better fighting force.

A turning point came on February 23, 1778, with the arrival of Baron von Steuben. A veteran of the Prussian army and the Seven Years War, von Steuben came to America to serve as a volunteer in the revolution. He met with Congress with a letter of introduction from Benjamin Franklin, whom he had met in 1777 in France. Although von Steuben had never risen above the rank of captain in the Prussian army, Franklin's letter introduced him as "His Excellency, Lieutenant General von Steuben, Apostle of Frederick the Great," and after being presented with this title to George Washington at Valley Forge and making a positive impression upon General Washington, von Steuben was appointed Inspector General.

General von Steuben lived up to his new title. Impressed with the spirit of the Continental army—he was quoted as saying, "no European army could have held together in such circumstances"—von Steuben set about writing drills for them. Because each state's troops used different drills and maneuvers, there was no standard method. He did not write or speak English, yet von Steuben nevertheless drafted a unified military code, in French, which his secretary translated into English. There were no translation issues with the drills themselves, which the soldiers learned quickly and well. Von Steuben worked with the troops personally and became popular among the soldiers. As maneuvers grew more orderly, morale increased, and the army's outlook improved day by day. They were finding a way.

On May 6, 1778, news came that the French had formally recognized the United States as a sovereign power and agreed to become its ally in the war. To celebrate, General von Steuben led the Continental army in a public display of their marching skills, which impressed soldiers, officers, and civilians alike. They had come a long way in just a few short months.[3]

A Will Tested, a Way Found

The decision to march to Valley Forge and stand for the "moral rightness of the American cause," a decision driven by willpower, came before the promising developments of the spring of 1778. Washington and his men acted in pursuit of a noble cause and were determined to find ways to support it.

Each step that winter—the building of huts, the construction of trenches, the arrival of General von Steuben, his uniform professional training regimen, the news of the French alliance—correlated with increased morale. With each small victory, the men began to see a path to success, and their resolve grew ever stronger. Willpower led to waypower, and waypower led to a way.

---

[3]Valley Forge National Historical Park, www.nps.gov/vafo/historyculture/vonsteuben.htm.

Shortly after leaving Valley Forge, on June 28, 1778, the Continental army engaged the British at the Battle of Monmouth and forced the British from the field. Peace would not be declared until 1783, but the army had survived a test of its will, and a corner had been turned.

Motivation: The Foundation of Willpower

Strong willpower is rooted in strong motivation. As we saw in Chapter 2, motivation is the reason behind actions and decisions; it can be internal, known as intrinsic motivation, or external, known as extrinsic motivation. Both types of motivation can help you reach your goals.

Intrinsic motivation is tied to an inner desire—an emotional energy, a will to persist, a belief in a noble cause. When we are driven by an intrinsic motivation, we are not concerned with awards or recognition because we don't need those incentives to act. The will of Washington's army was fed by an intrinsic motivation for freedom, independence, and the right to enjoy the blessings of liberty. Intrinsic motivation can lead to external benefits, of course, but its primary driving force is always something close to the heart.

However, if there were soldiers who signed on primarily in the hope of achieving personal glory such as financial reward or military honors, those soldiers would have been driven by an extrinsic motivation, a motivation validated by external recognition.

Intrinsic motivation and extrinsic motivation often work together to help propel you toward your goal. For example, soldiers and officers in the Continental army could well have been motivated by both the noble cause of freedom and the potential accolades that could come from extraordinary service. At different points throughout the campaign, they may have called on different motivations to help see them through difficult times.

The Herzberg Principle

Extensive research has been conducted on motivation and how it impacts performance—in the workplace and among college students. After examining workplace motivation, psychologist Frederick Herzberg concluded that *removing dissatisfaction does not lead to intrinsic motivation*. I call this the **Herzberg Principle**. Herzberg further states, "The factors leading to job satisfaction are separate and distinct from those that lead to job dissatisfaction." He contends that "the opposite of 'Satisfaction' is 'No Satisfaction,' and the opposite of 'Dissatisfaction' is 'No Dissatisfaction. . . . to eliminate factors that create job dissatisfaction can bring about peace, but not necessarily motivation."[4]

We saw this at work with the Continental army at Valley Forge. It's hard to imagine any of the soldiers expressing satisfaction with their living or working conditions when they first arrived—they were cold, hungry, and poorly

---

[4]Stephen P. Robbins, *Organizational Behavior*, 8th ed. (Upper Saddle River, NJ: Prentice Hall, 1998).

equipped—yet their dissatisfaction did not affect their motivation or desire to work hard for the cause. They were willing to endure poor conditions and maintain good spirits because they were intrinsically motivated. As conditions improved, they grew more satisfied with their environment and could more clearly see a path to their success, but that satisfaction did not impact their motivation—only their confidence.

To put this in a college perspective, addressing negative environmental aspects of your educational experience, such as dissatisfaction with cafeteria food, the parking situation, the cost of tuition, or your living arrangements, won't help your motivation—they'll just make you not dissatisfied. This can certainly make daily life easier and more pleasant, but it won't make you motivated. Motivation must come from somewhere else, either internally or externally.

Journal Entry: Dissatisfaction vs. Satisfaction

The table in Figure 4.1 identifies the factors Herzberg used when categorizing issues of satisfaction and dissatisfaction in the workplace. You can see that the factors are not direct opposites of each other.

To the right of the factors Herzberg identifies, list some areas in which you have been or currently are the most dissatisfied with your college experience and those areas in which you are the most satisfied. Then answer the following questions in your journal:

- How do the factors that you are dissatisfied with in your college experience affect your motivation to succeed in college?

- What is the connection between the factors with which you are the most satisfied and your motivation to succeed in college?

- Comparing the workplace lists with your lists, what do you notice? What conclusions can you draw about motivation?

FIGURE 4.1   Herberg's Satisfaction/Dissatisfaction Characteristics

Herzberg's Categories from the Workplace		Your College Experience	
Factors Characterizing Events That Lead to Extreme Dissatisfaction	Factors Characterizing Events That Lead to Extreme Satisfaction	Factors Characterizing Events That Are Extremely Dissatisfying	Factors Characterizing Events That Are Extremely Satisfying
Company police and administration	Achievement	1.	1.
Supervision	Recognition	2.	2.
Relation with supervisor	Work itself	3.	3.
Work conditions	Responsibility	4.	4.
Salary	Advancement	5.	5.
	Growth	6.	6.

The Alfie Kohn Principle

Another researcher who has examined motivation is the educational author Alfie Kohn. He has written nearly a dozen books on human behavior, education, and parenting, and his research and controversial approaches to teaching in his book *Punished by Rewards: The Trouble with Gold Stars, Incentive Plans, A's, Praise, and Other Bribes* overlap with Herzberg's motivational theory.[5] The basis of Kohn's theory in this book, which I have termed the **Alfie Kohn Principle**, is this: *External rewards may bring short-term extrinsic motivation, but they work against long-term intrinsic motivation.* Kohn asserts that the educational system has failed our nation's children by giving them awards for nearly everything—beginning with gold stars in elementary school. He contends that the fixation with extrinsic rewards has stifled intrinsic motivation and proposes that grades and competition be replaced with cooperative learning. Kohn's work is another reminder that a wide variety of educators are questioning the focus on and use of extrinsic motivation in education.

Journal Entry: Your Intrinsic and Extrinsic Motivation

Think back through your academic career, going back all the way to elementary school, and in your journal, answer the following questions:

- What extrinsic rewards did you receive for your achievements?

- How did those rewards make you feel?

- What was the long-term impact of those extrinsic rewards on your motivation to learn and your academic success?

- In your school years, what intrinsically motivated you?

- Which type of motivation has been more influential on you throughout your schooling? Which is more influential on you now? Why?

What Keeps Students in College?

The premise of this book is that your intrinsic motivation can sustain you in college, regardless of your dissatisfaction with some aspects of college. I once asked my colleague Scott Carroll how he'd develop a program to keep students in college.

"I would take all that money schools spend on 'retention' programs," he said, "and as part of pre-orientation, I'd buy hammers for all incoming students, and have them roof buildings for two weeks in mid-August. In my experience, a good roofing job in hot weather will do more to keep students in college than just about anything else you can do." Though his was a tongue-in-cheek response, and I know Scott certainly meant no disrespect to roofers, there's an undeniable truth in it: Once you've suffered through a job that holds no long-term

---

[5]Alfie Kohn, *Punished by Rewards: The Trouble with Gold Stars, Incentive Plans, A's, Praise, and Other Bribes* (New York: Houghton Mifflin, 1993). For his comments on Herzberg, see pp. 133–34.

appeal to you, it becomes much easier to find the willpower to graduate from college so you won't have to take a job like that ever again.

Once the willpower to graduate is in place, the waypower is more likely to follow: You're more likely to seek out resources and support, more likely to develop better study habits, and more likely to identify ways that will help you get where you want to go.

While I see the wisdom in Scott's suggestion to distribute hammers to incoming students, I've found that there are other tools that can be equally effective in helping keep students in school. The tools I use don't fit as easily in a tool belt, and they may take longer to understand completely, but once students grasp what these tools can do, they can take an active role in working to build their own futures.

My tool preferences are associated with basic student success principles. These principles have been developed through many years and a great deal of research, but I think you'll agree that many of them make common sense. Below are a few of these key principles.

1. Students who understand their general life purpose are highly likely to complete college, regardless of obstacles. (This might explain how you came to be reading this text.)

2. Students who are passionate about a cause are highly likely to complete college because they realize the value and necessity of a college degree in helping with such causes in the long term. (Think about the impact service learning has had on your academic learning.)

3. Students decide within the first two weeks of college if they will remain in college. (Think about orientation and your first couple of weeks of classes—what did you experience that helped you to adjust to your new environment?)

4. Quality interaction with a professor or staff person during the first weeks of college is critical in determining the success of a student, especially for underrepresented populations. (How many meetings did you have with advisors, RAs, peer mentors, or professors in the first few weeks of your first term? Do you think all those meetings were random or intentional?)

5. A common experience among first-year students helps build unity among new students, which enhances their chances of success. (Is there a common course at your college for all new students or a common group activity during orientation?)

6. Peer leadership helps engage students and assists with their learning and adjustment. (Do any of your courses use student helpers? Do these students seem more approachable than the professor?)

Part of the thinking behind the student satisfaction movement is that "unhappy customers don't come back." I refuse to think of you as a customer—you're a student. And while you care, and should care, about issues of satisfaction like food quality and parking availability, removing environmental dissatisfactions won't help you succeed in college, or in life. Connecting with something that inspires and moves you—in other words, being intrinsically motivated—will.

RISE to the Challenge: Finding Your Waypower

I sincerely hope you don't ever face the kinds of challenges George Washington faced, but I have no doubt you will face many of your own challenges throughout your college career and throughout your life. While these challenges may feel intimidating or overwhelming, they will also be something else: an opportunity.

Challenges are trials that invite you to learn new knowledge, develop new skills, and rethink old habits. Challenges test your resolve, reveal your strengths and weaknesses, and forge your character. Challenges help us find new and better ways forward. When we embrace challenges rather than fear them, they can become defining experiences in our lives.

How do you turn a challenge from a negative to a positive? You **RISE** to it.

Recognize the reality of the challenge. What's really happening here? Is this challenge the result of circumstances beyond your control, or is it a situation you've created? Is this a true challenge worthy of your best energies, or is it an inconvenience or annoyance simply sparking complaint? If you want to rise to—and above—a challenge, you must fully understand its context, causes, and constraints and be honest with yourself and others about what's at stake.

Identify opportunities. As daunting as this challenge may immediately seem, what positive outcomes can you imagine from overcoming it? How does this challenge connect with your Life Wedge or with a noble cause that drives you? These connections may not be obvious, but identifying how overcoming this challenge links to achieving a life goal will help you find the focus, drive, and discipline needed to persist. It will help you find a way.

Strategize a way forward. To overcome a challenge, you have to have a plan—challenges are rarely bested by accident. As you develop your strategy, be specific: What specific obstacles lie in your way? What specific tasks will be needed to move forward? What specific resources will you need to enlist? If you've done your job in the first two steps of this process, you've identified what led to the situation in which you find yourself; in this step, you're developing a specific plan that leads out of it.

Execute your strategy. This step may seem obvious, or even redundant—after all, if you've got a strategy, you're almost there, right? Not so fast. A plan for success isn't the same as success itself; many a great strategy has gone unexecuted, never seeing a life past the paper on which it was printed. To rise to the challenge and not fall to it, you must execute. What does execution mean? To borrow a phrase from Nike, it means, "Just do it." If your strategy includes specific tasks, it means doing them—taking the time each day to do what you've said is important to do. Execution is doing the little things that must be done to accomplish the big things.

Washington's RISE at Valley Forge

With this model in mind, let's review how George Washington and the Continental army met the challenges that faced them in the winter of 1777-1778.

Recognize the reality of the challenge. Washington knew the Continental army needed to regroup and would need to get better and stronger if they were to defeat the British the following spring. While they chose to spend the winter at Valley Forge because of its strategic advantages, they were realistic about the logistical challenges they would face there. Washington was honest with himself and his troops about the difficulties of their situation, but by reminding his soldiers of their noble cause and helping them understand the tasks needed to achieve their goals, he was able to rally them behind him.

Identify opportunities. As limited as resources were upon arrival at Valley Forge, Washington knew that if his men could get warm, get fed, and get healthy, their strength would increase and their confidence would grow. Thus, examining the resources available to them and identifying opportunities to fortify the troops, the leaders of the Continental army quickly set about building huts, securing supplies, and taking care of the basics. As the army overcame these immediate challenges, they linked their small victories with the larger victory they hoped to attain, and it grew easier and easier for them to persist.

Strategize a way forward. The arrival of General von Steuben was a turning point for the Continental army because of his impact on their strategy—their approach to becoming a better fighting force. Von Steuben immediately understood the need for disciplined, organized regiments and developed a specific plan to train the troops.

Execute your strategy. As good as those drills looked on paper, what made them and the strategy effective was General von Steuben's willingness to work directly with the troops in a hands-on way every day. With each new round of drills, soldiers became more skilled, until the techniques and habits they needed for success became second nature, and they were ready to execute them on the battlefield.

From Shepherd to Sage

At the time of his retirement from Miami University (Ohio) in 2005, Edwin Yamauchi was one of the world's leading authorities on ancient history. But first, he was a shepherd.

After being ostracized as a teenager by his Buddhist family in Hawaii because he chose to adopt the Christian faith, Edwin moved to the Christian Youth Farm and tended sheep. In those long stretches of solitude in which the sheep don't do very much, he also studied the Bible—but not simply in the normal way you might expect. He gathered inner-linear Bibles from local missionaries, which were like two books in one: the same passage was printed on opposing pages, but in two different languages. By knowing one of the languages, he could learn the other.

Edwin adopted this habit out of a love for languages and the Bible, but it would also prove tremendously valuable to him in his career. He left Hawaii to study Biblical languages at the fledgling (and now defunct) Shelton College in New Jersey, and his language skills helped him gain admittance to a doctoral program at Brandeis University in Massachusetts, where he earned his Ph.D. in an unprecedented two years.

As far as he had come from his days in the field with grazing sheep, more obstacles awaited. Dr. Yamauchi began his teaching career at Rutgers University, but he was denied tenure there, which means that a committee of his peers assigned to review his application for permanent status voted not to keep him at Rutgers long term.

Disappointed by this setback but unwilling to give up on his dream of a career as a professor, Dr. Yamauchi took a new position at Miami, where he committed himself to expanding his knowledge of languages. At Miami University football games, he brought a handful of language cards and studied them at every stoppage of play—huddles, time outs, halftime, any opportunity he could find. When he mowed his lawn, he taped language cards to the handle. And on Wednesday afternoons immediately following his last class of the day, he left Oxford, Ohio, and drove straight to the Blegan Classical Library at the University of Cincinnati, where he would conduct research through the late hours, spend the night, and research again in the morning before returning back to the Miami campus.

Through his efforts, Dr. Yamauchi not only was awarded tenure at Miami, he became one of the world leaders in Biblical studies, publishing nearly 20 books and countless articles in the field. At his retirement party, the host shared with the few hundred students, former students, and colleagues in attendance that the planning team had tracked the total number of research languages in his publications. The tally was 26.

How did Dr. Yamauchi RISE to the challenges he faced? Let's take a look.

Recognize the reality of the challenge. Dr. Yamauchi recognized that if he hoped to move beyond his life as a shepherd, he needed a formal education. He also realized that he could take responsibility for his situation by teaching himself, which he did by reading the multilingual Bibles. When he had earned his Ph.D. and his challenge was to get tenure, he recognized where he needed to improve as a scholar and refused to blame anyone else for his circumstances.

Identify opportunities. Even as a teenage shepherd, he understood that a college and graduate degree were needed to teach at the college level and that his language skills would help him obtain and secure funding for his enrollment. He took advantage of the opportunities he had—for example, the long stretches of solitude inherent to the life of a shepherd—to develop his language skills.

Strategize a way forward. His strategy was targeted and specific. In his younger years, he knew the value of studying multilingual bibles, and in his older years, he emphasized continual learning of many, many languages and saw the benefits of researching primary texts. He knew all of these elements constituted a strategy that would help him achieve his goals.

Execute your strategy. As wise as his strategies were, the key was execution. It would have been easy to daydream while the sheep grazed, but instead he read. Nobody would've blamed him if he enjoyed the football games like any other fan, but he brought those language cards and studied them. He turned his strategy from a handful of ideas into a part of his daily life.

I was fortunate to share an office with Dr. Yamauchi while serving as his intern many years ago. To watch him daily was to catch an in-depth study of his sharp, narrow Life Wedge and to appreciate his efforts to rise to the challenges he faced throughout his lifetime.

RISE and Cheer

I have also been fortunate to observe this next example first-hand—he's my son.

Unlike George Washington and Edwin Yamauchi, **Jason (Tiller) Pattengale** is not a public figure. In fact, he's rather shy, and he's a little uneasy about the fact that I'm even sharing his story in a public forum like this. Yet he has overcome more than his share of personal obstacles, and though you may not know him, I'll bet you know someone like him.

When Jason was only six years old, his biological father was killed when a reckless teenager ambushed him, knocking him unconscious and into the river, where he drowned. Two years later, I married Jason's mother and adopted Jason and his two younger brothers; despite this tragedy, it seemed as though Jason would be able to live a fairly normal life.

Then he was diagnosed with Crohn's disease, a chronic digestive disorder that causes inflammation of the gastrointestinal tract. The abdominal pain from his Crohn's episodes often incapacitated him, and the treatment—surgeries, radical diets, and a daily fistful of pills—sometimes felt worse than the disease. At times during his first and last years of college, Jason went directly from the doctor's office to a final exam. Other times he took six-hour round trips for special treatments to stabilize the Crohn's symptoms. Several times, his bouts were so serious that he lost as much as 30 pounds in a stretch. During his senior year, when things were at their worst, he had to move home and sometimes had to be carried around the house. That year, he handled most of his homework online and secured multiple unavoidable incompletes. Crohn's was an unrelenting, unwelcome roommate that would just not go away.

Yet as awful as his Crohn's was at times, Jason never let it define his college experience. He was too busy being a happy, involved college student.

Although his condition kept him from participating in contact sports like soccer (which he played, and loved, in high school), he had set a goal for himself to play college sports. With soccer off the table, he turned to varsity cheerleading—which practiced at 6:30 a.m., two days a week; 6:00 p.m., two other days a week; and again on Saturdays.

But the rigorous practice schedule merely served to weed out the uncommitted. Jason was not among those ranks. He loved the sport, he loved his team, and he loved the back flips.

His cheer team became nationally ranked, and his peers elected him team captain. In the spring of his senior year, the coaches recognized Jason for being the only one in his class to earn a varsity letter all four years.

Crohn's never released its grip—Jason visited three surgeons in the four weeks leading up to his college graduation, which he almost missed. He had six feet of his intestine surgically removed and endured long periods hooked to a Remicade bag.

But he made it. As you might imagine, there was not a dry eye among the Pattengale family when Jason walked across the graduation platform, and we shared those tears of joy with many friends. In fact, I get emotional just retelling the story.

Every parent is proud of a child who graduates from college. But when you have a son who can RISE to the challenge like Jason did, it's extra special.

Recognize the reality of the challenge. Jason was realistic about his Crohn's diagnosis. He wasn't exactly thrilled with it, but he acknowledged that it would affect his life. He knew he had to take the treatment seriously, and he recognized the danger he would face if he kept playing a contact sport like soccer.

Identify opportunities. While Crohn's would keep him from doing some things, Jason was determined not to let it keep him from doing everything. It closed the door to soccer, but it opened the door to cheerleading, a sport he might not have considered otherwise. Jason saw the opportunities for fun, exercise, and camaraderie that cheerleading offered and dove right in.

Strategize a way forward. Participating in cheerleading meant adhering to a structured practice schedule. Living with Crohn's meant establishing a treatment routine and taking his diet seriously. Succeeding academically meant balancing class work, cheerleading, and Crohn's. To do all this, Jason was meticulous about planning and scheduling, which helped him manage his time, his schoolwork, and his health.

Execute your strategy. Mapping out a routine is one thing. When that routine includes 6:30 a.m. cheerleading practices, and you're a college student, living that routine can be another thing altogether. But while getting out of bed was harder on some days than others, Jason found that the structure he built became a benefit rather than a burden. Because he executed his plan, day after day, week after week, his full days left him not tired, but fulfilled.

In rising to the challenges presented to him by Crohn's disease, Jason not only graduated from college, he made the most of his brief time on campus. While it would have been easy to retreat, he became socially engaged. While it would have been understandable if he'd just kept his head down and focused only on schoolwork and survival, he kept his head up and forged lifelong friendships, learning valuable leadership skills along the way. Although his days of doing back flips are over, I'm happy to report he no longer has to wear a colostomy bag either, and he now works at a wellness center, where he helps other people overcome physical setbacks and stay healthy.

Could I be more proud of him? It's certainly possible. But right now, it's pretty hard to imagine how.

Journal Entry: RISE to Your Challenge

Now that you've seen the RISE model at work with several examples, think about how you can apply it to a challenge you face. In the next section, we'll talk more about different kinds of challenges you might encounter at college, but before getting there, take a few moments to think about the first challenge that comes to mind. Is it a public challenge or a private one? Is it a new challenge or one you've struggled with for a while now?

Once you've identified your personal challenge, work through each of the steps of the RISE model with that challenge in mind—and take the first steps toward overcoming it.

Challenges All College Students Face

Jason's story of overcoming a major health challenge is inspiring. But even if your challenge isn't as monumental as his, that doesn't make it any less valid of a challenge. While many college students do face challenges as daunting as Jason's, nobody graduates from college without struggling with challenges of their own, often many at the same time. You undoubtedly already know that these challenges can have major consequences on your academic and personal lives.

As we examine the challenges that all college students face, keep in mind the role of intrinsic motivation—that genuine internal drive that leads you to pursue actions for their inherent value. No matter the nature of the challenge you may face, finding intrinsic motivation—whether a link to a cause, a commitment to an ideal, or a personal belief that what you're doing is simply worth doing—can help you RISE to that challenge.

Common College Challenges

Understanding the kinds of challenges you may be faced with is a critical first step in overcoming them. Let's take a look at some challenges common to all college students, and then we'll examine some additional challenges that may be unfamiliar to you.

1. **Personal:** Being away at college doesn't mean you can press a pause button on family crises back home, and situations that affect our families always affect us. Equally demanding of our focus and energies are romantic challenges; when we have problems in a dating relationship, everything can become a blur.

2. **Physical**: Lack of sleep, lack of exercise, constant stress and busyness, poor diet, alcohol use, and close quarters through which colds travel quickly all contribute to sluggish, worn-out students. The campus environment facilitates and often encourages this type of physical self-abuse, and the results can be significant: excessive absences and tardiness, sleeping through tests, dozing in class, poor information retention and class participation, and more.

3. **Financial**: Everyone acknowledges the high cost of college, but that doesn't make the financial reality of being a college student any less difficult. Every semester brings new syllabi with new textbooks to purchase and a big new bill at the bookstore. And while most people focus on the big-ticket items such as tuition, room, and board, small expenses like laundry or lunch can be stressful. This stress can grow if you're struggling to mesh work hours with class hours to generate sufficient income.

4. **Logistical**: With each year, we become more reliant on technology, which subjects us to greater potential challenges: problems getting online, problems accessing electronic course materials, and good old hardware and software problems. Another type of logistical challenge is transportation—fighting traffic getting to or from campus, finding a place to park close to class, getting home during breaks, and negotiating public transit schedules, in addition to the cost factors associated with each.

5. **Cultural**: We often don't think about our own culture until we realize it's in conflict with the culture around us. This might mean being an older student among younger students, holding minority political views, following ethnic traditions not considered by administrators or peers, or gender issues that might come up from situations such as being a woman in a male-dominated engineering program or a man in a female-dominated nursing program.

6. **Relational**: By their very nature, relationships can be challenging. Challenges in this category can include getting along with your roommate, interacting with fellow students in a commuter lounge, or even having trouble relating to a professor or teaching assistant.

Journal Entry: Recognizing the Challenge

Certainly you recognize some of the above challenges as your own, and you know how they create extra work and concern for you as you pursue specific tasks within your Life Wedge. In your journal, choose two types of challenges listed above and answer the following questions related to each:

- How do I relate to this challenge?

- How is my situation different from peers who face this challenge?

Formal Challenges

Most of us can relate to those common challenges because most of us have faced most of them, and people are comfortable sharing the frustrations that come from many of these challenges: moaning about being tired, groaning about the cost of books, venting about the wireless signal going down or how long it took to find a place to park.

But many college students face challenges that, while much less public and well-known, are equally common. These challenges often come with an official diagnosis, which helps students facing these challenges get help through formal, established channels. There are two major types of these challenges: official medical challenges and official challenges contributing to at-risk status.

To determine which situations or conditions qualify as "official" challenges, universities consult medical and government charts. Universities also respond to these challenges by establishing a variety of offices and programs for those diagnosed with these challenges. These may be called the Office of Student Support Services, Office of Student Success, or Office for Student Disabilities.

For many of these challenges, the student can choose whether to solicit assistance or inform others. However, if students do not get an official diagnosis for a challenge or identify themselves to the university, they usually do not qualify for certain types of assistance, nor do they benefit from special arrangements that can help them complete their coursework such as extra time on tests or note-taking assistance. After reading through the lists below, if you feel you are facing one of these official challenges, be sure to reach out to the appropriate support office on your campus.

Official Medical Challenges

- **Sight and Hearing Challenges.** This includes students with vision at a legally blind or hearing at a legally deaf level. Many students who are considered legally blind are not totally blind, but they cannot read at a normal level without alternate means or assistance.

- **Learning Challenges.** The list of diagnosed challenges to the learning process is long and includes reading problems such as dyslexia; speech and language disorders that complicate the communication process; and learning disabilities (sometimes referred to as *learning differences*), which have nothing to do with intelligence but rather with how information is processed.

- **Behavior Challenges.** While ADD/ADHD (attention deficit disorder/attention deficit hyperactivity disorder) is the most common challenge in this category, numerous other challenges that affect behavior (depression, autism, sleep apnea, and others) are also included.

- **Physical Challenges.** These range from loss of mobility or access, such as someone who is paraplegic or an amputee, to conditions such as cerebral palsy, cancer, autoimmune diseases, or gastrointestinal disorders.

Official Challenges Contributing to At-Risk Status

Challenges do not discriminate: They occur to people at all socioeconomic levels, of all races, and of all faith traditions. Someone financially well-off may suffer from Crohn's disease, a star athlete may deal with clinical depression, and a gifted mathematician may struggle with dyslexia. No one is immune.

However, research has shown a statistical correlation between certain factors that college students face and the likelihood of graduating from college. Students who face any of the following challenges are considered "at-risk" because they generally have more to overcome than other students; according to hundreds of statistical studies with large groups of students, the odds against them are higher than average. This doesn't mean those odds can't be overcome, of course; it just means that universities take extra care to help students most likely in need of assistance.

- **Economic Challenges.** This challenge is identified in relation to a student's family income. Like the amount of aid rewarded through the Pell Grant and the FAFSA calculations, some federal programs identify "at-risk" as those meeting the federal poverty guidelines, or some percentage of a related formula. Figure 4.2 provides a frame of reference. Poverty level implies minimal living conditions, beyond affording a house, movies, or paying for a child's wedding.

- **Underrepresented Challenge.** Numerous studies reveal that minority students and other underrepresented populations face special challenges and dynamics in the campus environment, ranging from social adaptations, learning styles, support groups, racism (intentional and unintentional), literary references, communication patterns, use of idioms, and many others.

- **First-Generation Challenge.** Many students enter college without the benefit of parental experience in higher education. "First-generation" literally means that a student is the first generation in his or her family to go to college—neither parent is a college graduate. Studies show a direct

FIGURE 4.2 2006 HHS Poverty Guidelines

Persons in Family or Household	48 Contiguous States and D.C.	Alaska	Hawaii
1	$ 9,800	$12,250	$11,270
2	13,200	16,500	15,180
3	16,600	20,750	19,090
4	20,000	25,000	23,000
5	23,400	29,250	26,910
6	26,800	33,500	30,820
7	30,200	37,750	34,730
8	33,600	42,000	38,640
For each additional person, add	3,400	4,250	3,910

SOURCE: *Federal Register* 71, no. 15 (January 24, 2006), pp. 3848–49.

correlation between this dynamic and the percentage of those who graduate from college (or who are "successful").

Reaching Out for Help

Although struggling with challenges is an unavoidable part of being a college student—not to mention being a human being—and most campuses offer an abundance of resources for support and assistance, many college students are reluctant to reach out for help. Sometimes it's a matter of pride; they think they can and should be able to get through their struggles on their own. Sometimes it's a matter of trust; they might ask friends or family for advice, but they just don't trust people in the "administration," even though those people are professionally trained in helping students. Other times it's arrogance; they think those student services and student counseling offices are for "other" people, people with "real problems," but not them. And still other times, people don't reach out for help because they're afraid that asking for help might mean that they really do have problems, and they don't want to admit that, to themselves or to anyone else.

But consider this: If you're struggling with a challenge—whether a common challenge or an "official" one—and you haven't at least explored those campus resources to see what they have to offer, are you really doing everything you can to succeed? Are you doing everything you can to sharpen your Life Wedge? Or are you just being stubborn?

Let me offer another way to think about those resources: You're already paying for them. Now, if you paid a membership fee to belong to a fitness club, and that club offered free massage therapy services, with a licensed massage therapist, to help with your physical well-being and support your training efforts, would you take advantage of that resource?

I know I would. And while a visit to the Office of Student Support Services may not be quite as relaxing as a visit to the massage therapist, I encourage you to think of what they offer there as a free service to help with your *mental* well-being and support your *academic* efforts.

Journal Entry: Support Systems

As we've discussed in this chapter, there are no shortages of challenges facing you as a college student. But what about support systems? Take a moment to consider whom you turn to when you are struggling with challenges, and then answer the questions below in your journal.

- When struggling with a challenge, whom have you turned to for support in the past? Why have you turned to that person or organization? How effectively has that person or organization provided support? What additional support do you wish you had when struggling with a challenge?

- What support systems exist on your campus that you have not used? What do you know about them? Why have you not used them before? Do you know people on your campus who have used any of those services? If so, what was their experience? Would you consider using one of these services in the future? Why or why not?

Chapter 4 Review

SUMMARY OF MAJOR CONCEPTS

- Motivation drives willpower, and motivation can be internal (intrinsic) or external (extrinsic).

- Waypower naturally flows from willpower; if you have the will to achieve something, you will work to find ways that will help you.

- Removing dissatisfaction doesn't make you satisfied; neither does it make you successful or provide motivation.

- External rewards are usually short-term motivators, but intrinsic motivation has the potential to last a lifetime.

- Challenges in college and life are unavoidable; the key is whether you rise to the challenge or fall to it.

KEY TERMS

willpower   the personal strength and discipline, rooted in strong motivation, to carry out your decisions or plans.

waypower   the path toward a goal, by which the exertion of willpower helps you see opportunities and find resources and support.

Herzberg Principle   the principle, based on the research of Frederick Herzberg, that states that removing dissatisfaction does not lead to intrinsic motivation.

Alfie Kohn Principle   the principle, based on the research of Alfie Kohn, that states that external rewards may bring about short-term extrinsic motivation, but they work against long-term intrinsic motivation.

RISE Model   a model used to respond to challenges, which includes the following steps: **Recognize** the reality of the challenge; **Identify** opportunities; **Strategize** a way forward; and **Execute** your strategy.

APPLICATION EXERCISE

Willpower and Waypower

In this chapter, we discussed willpower and waypower and how the two work together. In this exercise, you're going to consider the willpower and waypower needed to help you achieve one of the goals that you set earlier.

First, choose an important goal that you have established for yourself. This can be an academic goal, a professional goal, or a personal goal. Second, write out the goal in the column on the left. In the middle column, write down five specific examples of willpower (such as "Review class notes each day after class for 15 minutes") you will need to demonstrate to achieve this goal. Then, in the column on the right, write down five examples of waypower that you will need to achieve this goal. These may be finding a tutor or a mentor or some other example that will work in partnership with your willpower to help you achieve your goal.

Goal	Examples of willpower you will need to achieve this goal	Examples of waypower you will need to achieve this goal
	1.	1.
	2.	2.
	3.	3.
	4.	4.
	5.	5.

REMINDER

Keep sketching wedges as you consider the content of each chapter. For example, as you read about concepts like "waypower" look at a simple representation of your Ideal Wedge (literally, a few lines and key words) and reflect on your own plans. Another example is in the "RISE and Cheer" section, as you read about Jason; what are some of the routines that you could write in the RISE acronym alongside your sketch? Or, at the least, ones you can envision as you think about the Life Wedge diagram?

CHAPTER 5

5 Hope and Perseverance

The Price of Freedom

Although he had already served nearly 10 years in prison, Nelson Mandela was prepared to serve more. Offered a release in 1971 from the Robben Island Prison, seven kilometers off the coast of South Africa, where he had been imprisoned since 1962, Mandela refused.

He rejected the offer from his jailers because personal freedom had never been his priority. Mandela was aiming for a larger goal: the end of apartheid, and, with it, freedom for all citizens of his native South Africa.

Since 1948, the government of South Africa had been engaged in apartheid, the practice of segregation that divided the country by race. The word itself derived from the Afrikaans term "apartness," and that apartness was implemented by the Afrikaner National Party (dominated by those of Dutch descent) to secure power and control. Not only did the laws of apartheid divide the country, they also resettled people according to race and gave white citizens—only 20 percent of the population—economic, educational, and political privileges. It was essentially legalized, state-sanctioned racism.

A Lifetime of Struggle and Perseverance

Even before the implementation of apartheid, life was difficult for blacks in South Africa. In 1913, the Natives Land Act was introduced, which prevented blacks (except those living in Cape Province) from buying, or even renting, land outside of designated reserves. As a result, Mandela, who was born in 1918, was engaged in the struggle for equal rights his whole life.

At the University College of Fort Hare, he was suspended from school for joining in a protest boycott. By 1944, Mandela and close associates formed the African National Conference Youth League to address civil equity issues. Mandela helped the leaders draft the important Program of Action in 1949, a year after the all-white elections voted in the National Party on the apartheid platform. When in 1952 the African National Congress (ANC) launched its Campaign for the Defiance of Unjust Laws, a mass civil disobedience campaign, Mandela was elected National Volunteer-in-Chief.

94

That same year, Mandela and his friend Oliver Tambo, who would later become ANC National Chairman, opened the first black law firm in the country and began to help disenfranchised blacks fight the complicated racist laws. But soon the laws caught up with them, as the authorities determined they were in violation of land segregation legislation and demanded that they move their legal practice out of the city. This ruling made it more difficult for their clients to access them, but the clients still came, and Mandela and Tambo remained committed to their cause. Tambo explained the challenges they faced:

> To reach our desks each morning Nelson and I ran the gauntlet of patient queues of people overflowing from the chairs in the waiting room into the corridors. . . . To be landless [in South Africa] can be a crime, and weekly we interviewed the delegations of peasants who came to tell us how many generations their families had worked a little piece of land from which they were now being ejected. . . . To live in the wrong area can be a crime. . . . Our buff office files carried thousands of these stories and if, when we started our law partnership, we had not been rebels against apartheid, our experiences in our offices would have remedied the deficiency. We had risen to professional status in our community, but every case in court, every visit to the prisons to interview clients, reminded us of the humiliation and suffering burning into our people.

In 1960, the South African government banned the ANC, and in 1962, Mandela was arrested, tried, and sentenced to five years in prison for treason. The National Party tried him again in 1964 and sentenced him to a life term. During his opening statement to the Pretoria Supreme Court at the Rivonia Trial in April of 1964, Mandela declared:

> It is not true that the enfranchisement of all will result in racial domination. Political division, based on colour, is entirely artificial and, when it disappears, so will the domination of one colour group by another. The ANC has spent half a century fighting against racialism. When it triumphs it will not change that policy.
>
>   This then is what the ANC is fighting. Their struggle is a truly national one. It is a struggle of the African people, inspired by their own suffering and their own experience. It is a struggle for the right to live. During my lifetime I have dedicated myself to this struggle of the African people. I have fought against white domination, and I have fought against black domination. I have cherished the ideal of a democratic and free society in which all persons live together in harmony and with equal opportunities. It is an ideal, which I hope to live for and to achieve. But if needs be, it is an ideal for which I am prepared to die.

Mandela was offered release in 1971 if he would accept the policies of apartheid and renounce his previous stance. He was not interested in such a compromise. Considering what he had said at his trial seven years earlier, this came as no surprise.

Perseverance Rewarded

As he continued to serve his prison sentence, international support began to rally behind Mandela and his cause in the 1980s. In 1985, South Africa earned economic sanctions from the United States and Great Britain. However, while many whites within South Africa helped lead opposition to apartheid, and many international forces joined in this opposition, violence and serious oppression continued.

Economic and political pressures mounted as a result of strikes, violence, and repeated confrontations. Black South Africans finally found some support within their country in 1986 and in earnest in 1990 when President F. W. de Klerk began to dismantle apartheid and reinstate black political units, including the ANC. On February 11, 1990, after 27 years in prison, Mandela was released.

The next year, at the first national conference of the ANC since its ban 31 years earlier, Mandela was elected president.

In 1993, Mandela and de Klerk were awarded the Nobel Peace Prize "for their work for the peaceful termination of the apartheid regime, and for laying the foundations for a new, democratic South Africa."[1]

His acceptance speech afforded the world a glimpse of the motivation that fueled his perseverance all those years in jail. The following is an excerpt of that speech given at Oslo, Norway:

> This reward will not be measured in money. . . . It will and must be measured by the happiness and welfare of the children, at once the most vulnerable citizens in any society and the greatest of our treasures.
>
> The children must, at last, play in the open veld ["field"], no longer tortured by the pangs of hunger or ravaged by disease or threatened with the scourge of ignorance, molestation and abuse, and no longer required to engage in deeds whose gravity exceeds the demands of their tender years. . . .
>
> The reward of which we have spoken will and must also be measured by the happiness and welfare of the mothers and fathers of these children, who must walk the earth without fear of being robbed, killed for political or material profit, or spat upon because they are beggars.
>
> They too must be relieved of the heavy burden of despair, which they carry in their hearts, born of hunger, homelessness and unemployment.
>
> The value of that gift to all who have suffered will and must be measured by the happiness and welfare of all the people of our country, who will have torn down the inhuman walls that divide them. . . .
>
> Thus shall we live, because we will have created a society, which recognises that all people are born equal, with each entitled in equal measure to life, liberty, prosperity, human rights and good governance.

In 1994, 46 years after the institution of apartheid, truly open elections were held in South Africa, and Nelson Mandela became the nation's first democratically elected president.

---

[1]Presentation Speech, Francis Sejersted, Chairman of the Norwegian Nobel Committee, Nobelprize.org, http://nobelprize.org/nobel_prizes/peace/laureates/1993/presentation-speech.html.

The Mandela Principle

In the last chapter, we talked about challenges, both the big, intimidating, history-changing kind and the smaller, daily, faced-by-every-college-student-every-day kind. Nelson Mandela offers an example of the former kind of challenge, but his response to it illustrates a critical characteristic that marks the success stories of people facing all kinds of challenges: struggle.

The string of challenges that faced Mandela throughout his life seemed like it might never end. Each of them—the Natives Land Act, apartheid, his imprisonment, and many more—was yet another obstacle between him and his goal of achieving justice and equality for all citizens of South Africa. His response to those challenges was to work to find ways over, around, or through those obstacles. When no clear way was evident, he kept searching, kept working, kept investing time and effort. He brought others into the cause. He resisted the very notion of giving up or giving in. He kept struggling.

With a warrant out for his arrest, Mandela offered a press statement on June 26, 1961, that explained his plans to continue the fight against an unjust government. "The struggle is my life," he said.[2] For Mandela, the struggle was inseparable from the goal because the struggle was his way to the goal. No matter how difficult it seemed—and during those 27 years in prison, it must have seemed incredibly difficult at times—his dream was always stronger than the struggle.

To overcome all those challenges and to endure through all those years of struggle, Mandela applied what I like to call the **Mandela Principle**:

> *No matter the length of the journey, perseverance is necessary to endure the struggle and reach the end. The right purpose makes perseverance possible.*

No matter your journey—to graduate from college, to achieve a career goal, to accomplish a personal objective—you need the sustained commitment that comes from perseverance to see you through to the end. And the clearer and more powerful that end is—the more compelling the purpose that guides your efforts—the stronger your perseverance is bound to be.

Journal Entry: Struggle and Perseverance

You don't need to face challenges as daunting as apartheid or pursue a cause as noble as racial justice to take valuable lessons from Mandela's story. In your journal, answer the following questions related to the discussion about struggle and perseverance.

- How would you describe the connection among Mandela's values, his goal, and his struggle to a friend who does not know Mandela's story?

- How would you describe the connection among your values, your goal(s), and your struggle to that same friend?

---

[2]"The struggle is my life," press statement, issued June 16, 1961, African National Congress Web site, http://www.anc.org.za/ancdocs/history/mandela/1960s/pr610626.html.

- What challenges have you faced (or are you currently facing) on the journey to your goal that have caused you to struggle? What have you learned from that struggle?

- How have you demonstrated perseverance in the face of struggle? How have you not?

- Would Mandela personally have been successful without the end of apartheid? Why? If yes, at what point did he have the assurance he was successful?

The Impact of Hope

In the face of long odds and intense struggle, what enabled Mandela to sustain his commitment to his cause? What fueled his perseverance?

He certainly had no shortage of intrinsic motivation—his immense willpower was evident throughout his life. But you could argue that his willpower, his stubborn refusal to sacrifice his principles, got him *into* prison. What kept him going through all those years behind bars and through all those years of apartheid? What made him believe those two brutal sentences would ever come to an end?

Even in his darkest hours, when things seemed most bleak, Mandela had hope.

He had hope that the will and the rights of the many could eventually champion the will and the rights of the few. He had hope that given enough time, his efforts and the efforts of his fellow freedom fighters could move the heavy boulder of oppression, even if it moved very, very slowly. And he had hope that, one way or another, justice would prevail.

Hope in this context, then, is not a simple concept. It's not the same as sitting around idly wishing for something to happen. We can compare hope to wishing the way we compared mature and immature dreams in Chapter 1: Wishing something might happen is like having an immature, undeveloped dream, while having hope in something you believe in is similar to having a mature dream.

Hope exhibits the same strengths as a mature dream when it is backed by specific goals and a deep reserve of willpower. Those two ingredients lead to waypower, the path to achieving those goals. Ultimately, hope is a belief rooted in something of substance—a cause, values, yourself, or even others.

When you look at hope through this lens, it's easy to understand the connection between hope and perseverance and how hope increases our likelihood of achieving our goal, whether it's ending apartheid or graduating from college. You also can see the role hope often plays in supporting, working for, or fighting for a noble cause.

The Hope Scale

The late Charles R. Snyder, with the help of his colleagues at the University of Kansas and other psychologists, studied the impact of hope on individuals and discovered ways to measure it. As outlined in Dr. Snyder's book *The Psychology of Hope*, these researchers found strong positive correlations between belief in one's ability to reach goals and actually reaching them.

One of the tools Dr. Snyder developed to measure hope is "The Hope Scale," the subject of dozens of reports he published throughout his career. While many researchers have used a wide array of instruments to ascertain the best way to help students succeed, and these surveys collectively contain hundreds of questions, Dr. Snyder's Hope Scale is brief. Despite its deceptive simplicity—it asks only eight questions—the Hope Scale has proven to produce valid results that help us understand levels of hope, a key aspect of intrinsic motivation.

The eight questions in the Hope Scale examine two aspects of hope: agency and pathways. Agency is a reflection of willpower, whereas pathways are an indication of waypower. You can review these concepts in Chapter 4 if needed.

Below are the eight questions that constitute the Hope Scale survey. Each question is associated with either agency (willpower) or pathways (waypower). Rate your response to each statement from 1 (definitely false) to 4 (definitely true). Then add up your answers to determine your Hope Score.

Journal Entry: Evaluating Your Hope Score

Once you have determined your score and tallied your overall Hope Score, answer the questions below in your journal:

- How do you feel about your overall Hope Score?

- Before evaluating yourself against the Hope Scale, would you have considered yourself a "high-hope" individual? Why or why not?

- How does your Hope Score align with your self-assessment?

- Did you score stronger on the agency questions or the pathways questions? Why do you think this is?

5.1   Dr. Snyder's "Hope Scale" Questionnaire

1. I can think of many ways to get out of a jam. (Pathways)

2. I energetically pursue my goals. (Agency)

3. There are lots of ways around any problem. (Pathways)

4. I can think of many ways to get the things in life that are most important to me. (Pathways)

5. Even when others get discouraged, I know I can find a way to solve the problem. (Pathways)

6. My past experiences have prepared me well for my future. (Agency)

7. I've been pretty successful in life. (Agency)

8. I meet the goals that I set for myself. (Agency)

Traits of High-Hope Individuals

According to research conducted by Dr. Snyder and his colleagues, "high-hope individuals"[3] typically:

- Can clearly conceptualize their goals *(conceptual trait)*.

- Can envision one major pathway to a desired goal and can generate alternative pathways, especially when the original one is blocked *(logistical trait)*.

- Perceive that they will actively employ pathways in pursuit of their goals *(emotional trait)*.

Since we know these traits have surfaced among thousands included in Dr. Snyder's studies, they present a good framework for examining our efforts in college. Let's take a look at each of these traits in greater detail.

Conceptual Trait

On our life journey, we're usually most aware of the parts of the path immediately behind us and immediately before us. By pausing to take a step back, look at the big picture, and think about the desired outcomes of that journey, we can better understand where we are in the context of where we're going.

Putting our efforts into a broader perspective in this way is known as **conceptualization**. In this process, we examine the path we've taken, observing our history of plans, actions, successes, and failures. We then identify patterns to better understand our journey and place our goals within this larger framework. Taking this longer view helps us apply our general knowledge to envision appropriate, mature goals.

Logistical Trait

Logistical action is putting into practice and managing what we have conceived. Think back to General von Steuben and the Continental army: Their broad goals involved defeating the British, and the logistics that helped them get there were the specific drills and training that transformed them into a disciplined, organized, and effective outfit.

Logistics are the calculation of what needs to take place in order to realize our goals. The very term comes from the Greco-Roman military ranks, where a *Logistikas* was charged with designing and overseeing supply routes. As you might guess from looking at the word itself, logistics shares the Greek root "logos" (which means, among other things, "reason") with logic, and we most commonly attempt to be logical by being reasonable and sequential—by processing a predictable rationale or path to a goal or answer. Logistics are about finding a way to match our will.

Dr. Snyder discovered that high-hope people have the ability to design or find such a route to their clearly conceptualized goals. They see a sequence of logical stops along the route that, when strung together, become a complete path toward their goal.

---

[3]C. R. Snyder, "To Hope, to Lose, and to Hope Again," *Journal of Personal and Interpersonal Loss* 1 (1996), pp. 1–16.

Although logistical thinking is often discounted as dry and dull, it demands creativity in problem solving, from developing intricate strategies to finding alternate routes when faced when unexpected challenges.

Emotional Trait

Even with goals that are clearly conceived and articulated and a logical path in front of you that has been outlined to achieve those goals, you still must take steps down that path actually to achieve those goals. As we all know from our own experience, some people will consistently take the steps they need to take, and some won't. Dr. Snyder's research says that high-hope people will. They're emotionally charged and have strong feelings about reaching the goals they have set. They tap into an inner desire to succeed—as we discussed in the last chapter, they apply an intrinsic motivation.

The flip side of this equation, of course, is that if we're not motivated, if we're not passionately driven to achieve our goals, it's much tougher to muster the perseverance we need, and we become more likely to succumb to the challenges we will inevitably face. To put it the way I phrased it in the very first chapter of this book, *the dream must be stronger than the struggle*. No matter how many plans we have in place, how many life skills we've honed, how high the grades we've obtained, or how much we've learned about our chosen career, if we don't have the desire to reach our goals, we won't.

Why do some people fail to take the path they've designed for themselves? Why can some people apply the conceptual trait and the logistical trait, but not the emotional trait? Many reasons exist, but I have often seen people lack emotional will because the goals they set were not their own or not ones about which they were truly passionate.

Journal Entry: Your Hope Traits

The three statements in this exercise correspond to the three traits we just discussed that Dr. Snyder identified in high-hope individuals. Read each statement, then circle the number that corresponds most closely with how often that statement reflects your behavior.

I Conceptualize Goals That Are Clear and Measurable—I'll know if I've Succeeded				
1	2	3	4	5
never	rarely	on occasion	usually	always

I Plan for Obtaining Results and Can Explain It to Others—I Can Assess if the Plan Is Working				
1	2	3	4	5
never	rarely	on occasion	usually	always

I Care Enough about My Goals to Act on My Plan—I Am Personally Invested				
1	2	3	4	5
never	rarely	on occasion	usually	always

In your journal, answer the following questions:

- How do the conceptual, logistical, and emotional traits work together?

- Pick one trait for which you did not circle "always." What would be the benefit of increasing the frequency of this behavior?

- What are some strategies (or pathways) you might take to increase the frequency of this behavior?

- In the light of Dr. Snyder's research about the benefits of being a "high-hope" person, what does your self-assessment help you discover about your approach to college?

Being Proactive or Passive

People often alternate between being **proactive** or **passive** in their lives. Being proactive means taking the initiative to make things happen, whereas being passive means allowing things to happen to you. You can choose to be proactive or passive in relation to all three of Dr. Snyder's basic components of hope—conceptual, logistical, and emotional.

Taking a proactive approach seems the one most likely to get things done, so why choose a passive approach? In actuality, most people don't actively *choose* the passive approach—the passive approach results when you don't choose to take a proactive one. Perhaps a better question then is: What keeps people from being proactive?

Sometimes people are afraid to make an active choice and take a come-what-may approach to goal-setting, planning, and the day-to-day decisions that determine actions and behaviors. This approach seems safer and easier in the short term because the risks of making the wrong decision are low. But in the long term, taking a passive approach is actually quite risky. If you fail to be proactive in making decisions and taking action, then you're letting other people, or the circumstances of the day, determine your future. While that may not seem painful or disappointing today, the more often you make that passive choice, the greater the chances you will be frustrated down the road by the choices made for you.

For example, let's say you think you want to go to law school, but you're not sure. Let's examine what a passive approach to this might look like, and what a proactive approach might look like.

Passive Punky

Imagine a passive first-year student named Punky. Passive Punky keeps telling herself, as well as her friends and family, that she might want to go to law school. That sounds reasonable enough; her friends all nod their heads agreeably when she says this, and her mother gets excited about having a lawyer in the family and the possibility of paying off student loans quickly. But Punky is passive about the conceptual component, so she doesn't really have a clear, mature goal of going to law school. It's more of a wish than a hope. She doesn't really know very much about what's involved in being at law school or getting into law school, just that you have to go there if you want to be a lawyer, and she figures she'll figure out the law school thing when the time comes.

Because she's been passive with the conceptual trait, it's easy to be passive with the logistical trait. After all, she doesn't really know what she needs to do to prepare herself for law school or a career in law, so how would she plan a strategy for those things? So she picks a major and takes a random sampling of classes, and she takes an off-campus job because it pays well and isn't too difficult or time-consuming. But it's not like she has an actual strategy about going to law school or anything. It still feels like years away.

Having taken such a passive approach to the conceptual and logistical aspects of goal setting, it's quite easy to be passive about the emotional component. No clear goal has been set, and no concrete plan has been developed that needs to be followed, so very little willpower or emotional investment is needed. Punky doesn't see too many challenges in front of her because she's just operating day-to-day.

When the end of her senior year rolls around, Punky thinks she better take the LSAT (Law School Admission Test) and start applying to law schools, but she's not well prepared for the test, and many of her peers began the application process months, if not years, earlier. She hasn't even visited law schools, so she really doesn't know what she's looking for in a program, let alone which school might offer what she wants, and she's already missed several deadlines to apply. Now in survival mode, she scours the Internet, looking for law schools with late application deadlines.

Proactive Pinky

In contrast, let's take a look at a proactive first-year student named Pinky. Proactive Pinky also arrived at college thinking she might want to go to law school. But before she commits herself to the time and cost of law school, and potentially a career in law, she wants to make sure that the goal aligns with her values and that she really knows what she's getting herself into. To help her goal mature, she talks with her academic advisor about classes that would help her succeed in law school. She visits a local law school and meets with an admissions director there, who gives her a tour, hands her informational materials, and invites her to sit in on a law school class. After the tour, which she enjoys, she goes home and reads through the brochures to learn more about being a law student, at that law school in particular. Her interest high; she sits in on the law school class, which she finds engaging and intriguing. She's excited about being a law student. After class, she goes to the front of the room, introduces herself, and thanks the professor. The professor then introduces her to a few students, who invite her to lunch, where the students talk honestly about what law school is like and what it takes to succeed there. Pinky is getting a clear sense of what she might be in for if she goes to law school. Her dream is maturing.

Now that the conceptual aspect of her goal is getting clearer, she realizes it's time to focus on the logistics. She schedules an appointment with a law school admissions counselor to discuss what classes she will need on her transcript to get into law school. She goes to the career center and asks about internships and summer jobs that are available at law firms so she can get hands-on experience in a legal environment. This experience not only will let her see life at a law firm up close, it also will help her make connections in the field and demonstrate to the admissions officers who eventually read her application that she understands the legal field and is serious about going to law school. She goes online to research law schools, their requirements, and costs. She plans visits to schools that interest her over her breaks. With each logistical step, her dream starts to become reality, and she gets more and more excited about it.

That excitement fuels the emotional trait—her willpower. When challenges come up throughout her collegiate career, she is motivated by her goal, which is clear and which she has been working toward since her freshman year. Her willpower and the waypower she has established through the strategy she developed help her persevere through tough times. She studies for several months for the LSAT in the fall of her junior year, but she is disappointed with her score because she isn't sure it's strong enough to get her into the schools she wants to attend. But because she has planned so well so far in advance, she has plenty of time to get a tutor and take the test again before the application season begins. She has invested so much into her dream, she's not going to let one disappointment on one standardized test hold her back. She prepares even better the second time and is less nervous on test day this time, and when her score comes back, she is pleased. By her senior year, her essays are written, her transcript is prepared, and she has a glowing recommendation from the law firm where she worked, as well as from several professors whom she impressed with her diligence and attitude. She submits all her applications early and eagerly awaits the replies.

At every step of the way, proactive Pinky thought ahead, took the more difficult path, and worked harder. Perhaps none of those sound appealing to you. But do you think passive Punky had a significantly more enjoyable college experience than Pinky did? Do you think Pinky perhaps enjoyed the positive feelings that came from knowing she was making steady progress toward her goal? In the end, even without knowing whether either of them got into law school, who would you rather be, Punky or Pinky?

Journal Entry: From Passive to Proactive

Take a moment to consider your scores on the sliding scale in the context of our discussion of being proactive or passive, and then, in your journal, answer the following questions.

- Think of a time when you have taken a passive approach, conceptually, logistically, or emotionally, and describe the situation. Why did you choose that passive approach?

- In this instance when you were passive, how did you feel about the result? How did being passive contribute to that result?

- Think of a time in which you took a proactive approach, and describe the situation. Why did you choose to be proactive?

- In this instance when you were proactive, how did you feel about the result? How did being proactive contribute to that result?

- What can you do to develop more proactive and less passive habits and behaviors?

The Other Side of Hope: Despair

Hope reflects a deep-seated belief in a positive future. But what happens when that belief is shaken, when optimism is hard to muster, and when you don't feel hopeful at all? We've all experienced those feelings at some point, and we're bound to feel them again. They're the opposite of hope: despair.

Despair reflects a loss of belief, in oneself, in a cause, in humanity. When you are feeling despair, the shadows of pessimism, negativity, and doubt lurk behind every thought. And when the odds are stacked against us, when it looks like only a fool would have hope, despair seems like a reasonable alternative. It seems rational and logical. Sometimes giving up just seems to make more sense than holding out hope.

People surely would have understood if Nelson Mandela opted for despair rather than hope. After all, his circumstances were oppressive, and the powerful National Party showed no signs of caving. Despair was arguably the most logical reaction to that situation. It was undoubtedly easier than hope.

Yet clearly, Mandela chose hope, in the face of conditions that to many people called for despair. How did he do that, for so many years?

From Despair to Hope: Lessons from High-Hope People

We've already discussed the power of perseverance and identified some traits that high-hope individuals exhibit. Dr. Snyder's research provides further insights in moving from despair to hope.

In his research, Dr. Snyder studied what "high-hope" people say and do. He concluded that the common process among people who successfully promote positive change or growth in their lives is that "they attempt to increase the sense of agency [willpower] and pathways [waypower] that [they] have for the goals in their lives."[4]

Based on these observations and on "research aimed at changing agency and pathways," he identified the following behaviors and activities for enhancing hope:

- Learn and practice positive self-talk about succeeding.

- Think about difficulties you encounter as reflecting a wrong strategy you pursued or decision you made, not a lack of talent on your part.

---

[4]C. R. Snyder, "Conceptualizing, Measuring, and Nurturing Hope," *Journal of Counseling and Development* 73 (January/February 1995), pp. 355–60.

- Think of goals and setbacks as challenges, not failures.

- When struggling, recall past successes, and remember what you did that worked.

- Read, watch, or listen to stories of how other people have succeeded, to inspire you and give you new ideas for pathways to success.

- Talk to friends about your goals, and ask for help and support.

- Find role models whom you can emulate or who may serve as a mentor, advisor, or guide; dozens of such role models are on your campus right now.

- Exercise physically, to remind yourself of how the body and mind are connected.

- Eat properly, to remind yourself of how good being well-fueled feels.

- Rest adequately, to recharge for the next active goal-directed output.

- Laugh at yourself, especially when you get stuck.

- Adjust your goals as needed because persistence in the face of absolute goal blockage can actually deflate agency and pathways.

- Reward yourself when you achieve small subgoals on the way to larger, long-term goals.

- Educate yourself for specific skills, and learn how to learn.

Adopting any of these behaviors or activities is, by definition, being proactive—further encouragement to shift your thinking away from a passive mindset. This list is also further evidence that hope is not some sort of flimsy, ethereal feeling. *Hope is a thinking process in which people exhibit willpower and waypower on the way to achieving their goals.*

The Tough Get Going

Throughout this chapter, we have discussed many strategies for strengthening hope and examined numerous theories and philosophies about perseverance and motivation. All of these are valuable.

But through the years, I have found one simple question that often trumps even those eight simple questions in Dr. Snyder's Hope Scale questionnaire when it comes to indicating someone's level of motivation. The question is this: How would you complete this sentence?

When the going gets tough, I _____.

The answer to this single question reveals so much about motivation, perseverance, and hope. How a student answers that one question can tell me a lot about that student's likelihood of graduating college.

So, what do you do when the going gets tough?

Chapter 5 Review

SUMMARY OF MAJOR CONCEPTS

- No matter the length of the journey, perseverance is necessary to endure the struggle and reach the end. The right purpose makes perseverance possible.

- Hope involves three key ingredients: willpower, goals, and a path to those goals.

- High-hope individuals can clearly conceptualize their goals, envision one major pathway to a desired goal, generate alternative pathways when the original is blocked, and perceive that they will actively employ pathways in pursuit of their goals.

- Being proactive means taking the initiative to make things happen, whereas being passive means allowing things to happen to you.

- Proactive, motivated people are more likely to succeed.

- You can practice specific behaviors to move from despair to hope.

KEY TERMS

Mandela Principle   the principle, named after South African leader Nelson Mandela, that states, "No matter the length of the journey, perseverance is necessary to endure the struggle and reach the end. The right purpose makes perseverance possible."

conceptualization   putting our efforts into a broader perspective by pausing to take a step back, look at the big picture, and think about the desired outcomes of that journey so that we can better understand where we are in the context of where we're going.

proactive   an approach in which you take the initiative to make things happen.

passive   an approach in which you sit back and allow things to happen to you.

APPLICATION EXERCISE

Characteristics of Hope and Despair

In reviewing the story of Nelson Mandela and the struggle for equality for all South Africans, you can undoubtedly identify multiple examples of hope and despair. For this exercise, choose a story that you know well—one that you know from history or from a book or movie—in which the people or characters involved face a wide range of difficulties and challenges. Books you might consider include the darker *Catcher in the Rye* or the hopeful *A Tree Grows in Brooklyn*.

With that story in mind, think about how the people involved respond to the challenges that arise. Do they exhibit hope? Despair? Both? Neither? What actions demonstrate these characteristics? In the table below, place at least three people from your chosen story into all of the categories that are appropriate (the same person might fall into multiple categories at different times in the story). Then, next to their names, write down the action or behavior they exhibited that led you to place them in that category.

People with Hope	Neither Hopeful nor in Despair	People in Despair

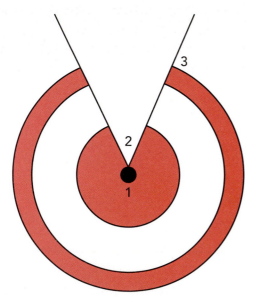

JOURNAL EXERCISE

Once you have completed this exercise, answer the following questions in your journal.

- Think about people with whom you interact at school or work. Identify one person who would fit in each of the three categories, and write down a behavior or action you have observed that explains why you placed that person there.

- Now think about yourself. Where would you place your own actions? How do you respond to the challenges of college or to a particular class?

REMINDER

As you continue to refine your Life Wedge, look at the willpower and waypower discussion. Are you being proactive in making progress toward your life goal, or are you just letting life come to you without taking the initiative? The willpower discussion begs the question: "Where are you taking the initiative in your own Life Wedge?" Can you identify proactive steps associated with the items in your Real Wedge? The waypower discussion is ripe with opportunities for reflection as well, as your entire Wedge reflects the pathways you have established to help you move toward your goal. Refine your Life Wedge as necessary in the light of this chapter's discussion.

Our Deepest Fear

Our deepest fear is not that we are inadequate.
Our deepest fear is that we are powerful beyond measure.
It is our light, not our darkness, that most frightens us.
We ask ourselves, "Who am I to be brilliant, gorgeous, talented and fabulous?"
Actually, who are you not to be?
You are a child of God. Your playing small doesn't serve the world.
There's nothing enlightened about shrinking so that other people won't feel insecure around you.
We were born to make manifest the glory of God that is within us.
It's not just in some of us; it's in everyone.
And as we let our own light shine, we unconsciously give other people permission to do the same.
As we are liberated from our own fear, our presence automatically liberates others.

Poem often cited as by Mandela, but actually
written by Marianne Williamson

6 Seeing the Big Picture

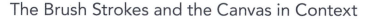

The Brush Strokes and the Canvas

Alone on a wall at the end of a long hall in the J. Paul Getty Museum, at the Getty Center in Los Angeles, hangs Vincent van Gogh's masterpiece *Irises*.

I knew I would find it there; in fact, *Irises* was the main reason *I* was there, and yet still I was unprepared for the effect of seeing this painting in person. I had seen countless reproductions—on posters, in books, on postcards, online—but when I turned the corner and saw the *Irises* themselves, my heart started thumping against my rib cage.

Sheepishly, as though van Gogh himself were standing next to it, I approached the canvas for a closer look. Standing just a few feet away, I saw something different. I saw clumps and uneven blobs of oil paint—something else the reproductions had never quite captured. I saw the brush strokes, van Gogh's creative building blocks, and I realized that while some were smooth and steady, some seemed sloppy, even random. The lone white iris on the left side of the painting, which from across the room had seemed to sing out from among its blue counterparts, to signal something significant and profound, looked up close like . . . a white iris. Kind of a clumpy one at that.

I took a few steps back to see the whole picture again, and the farther back I got, the less I saw a collection of individual brush strokes and the more I saw a work of art. I took a few steps forward again, examining those brush strokes and paint globs once more, wondering now in amazement not how those simple strokes added up to become those irises but how van Gogh knew *those* were the strokes he needed to create this masterwork. How could he see that so clearly?

For several minutes I did this dance with that canvas, forward and back, forward and back, needing to see both the canvas and the brush strokes, wanting to appreciate both the big picture and the small.

The Brush Strokes and the Canvas in Context

As powerful as it was to see *Irises* in person, would I have been quite as moved if I didn't know the story behind it?

Detail from *Irises*

Having studied van Gogh's life and art, I knew that *Irises* was one of the first pieces he painted from the asylum at Saint Paul-de-Mausole, in Saint-Rémy-de-Provence, in France. *Irises* captures a natural scene he saw in the asylum's garden. He had gone there in May 1889 to relax and recuperate after a mental breakdown and the famous incident in which he cut off part of his left ear. There, painting became part of van Gogh's therapy; he believed the process helped stave off his insanity. Over the course of what would be the final year of his life, van Gogh produced more than a hundred paintings.

I also knew that *Irises* was among the 10 most expensive paintings ever purchased. When it was sold at auction in 1987, the price was $53.9 million, at the time the most ever paid for a painting.

Story aside, the painting itself is a striking piece of art; I saw many children in the museum that day who likely didn't know the history of van Gogh or anything about auction prices but who nonetheless seemed to be able to appreciate the painting simply as something beautiful. Yet because I knew the history of the painting, and because I had seen it from up close and from far away, I appreciated this "simple" painting on three different levels.

At the core, the most elemental level, were those brush strokes. Having seen them up close, I now had an appreciation for both their apparent (though calculated) randomness and the craft behind them. I call this view the **Brush-Stroke Level**.

The next level, the **Canvas Level**, was farther away—a distance at which you could see the entire canvas as more than a collection of brush strokes and appreciate it as a complete painting. At this level, just about anyone can appreciate the painting, whether seeing it from the far end of the gallery or on a poster reprint.

The third level had less to do with the painting itself and more to do with the painting's place in history. Part of the reason my heart started pounding when I turned that corner was because I knew, before I even got a closer look at those individual brush strokes, that those brush strokes, those small movements made in an instant, were part of something much larger than even just a painting—they belonged to and were the building blocks of a body of work that dramatically influenced the art world and a life that became one of the most remarkable in modern times. The way van Gogh saw the world changed the way we see the world.

In other words, I saw those blobs and those brush strokes on that canvas, in that museum, in a much larger context: in the context of that painting, in the context of van Gogh's life, in the context of art, and in the context of history. Seeing the piece this way, then, to see it in the world and not just on the wall, is to see it at the **Context Level**.

Taken together, all three levels in this model—the Brush-Stroke Level, the Canvas Level, and the Context Level—make up the **Big Picture Approach**.

The Big Picture Approach: Art Imitates Life

This way of seeing, of appreciating at multiple levels in multiple contexts, is certainly not limited to works of art. Let's look back at a story we examined a few chapters ago, the Continental army's winter at Valley Forge, through this model.

For most people, "Valley Forge" summons images of George Washington, a cold winter, and the Revolutionary War. That basic understanding of Valley Forge is like the basic appreciation you might have of *Irises* from seeing the painting on a poster or in a coffee-table book. At this level, you know what the story is about, and you understand cultural references to it even if you don't fully understand all its historical implications. You're seeing it at the Canvas Level.

If you know your U.S. history fairly well, you understand the importance of the winter at Valley Forge to the American Revolution. The deeper your knowledge of world history, the greater your understanding of that winter's place in the larger arc of history and the greater your appreciation of the significance of the episode itself. In other words, the bigger the picture in which you see that episode, the greater the context you have for it, the more deeply you understand it. You're seeing it at the Context Level.

So where are the brush strokes? Think back to the drills General von Steuben taught the Continental army, every day on the field at Valley Forge. Think about the 2,000 huts built for shelter. Think about the miles of trenches, each dug with only a shovel, strain, and sweat. Without those individual actions—many of them tedious and repetitive, many of them unpleasant and painful, nearly all of them difficult—Valley Forge would be just another dot on the map in Pennsylvania, if that. But those actions, those brush strokes, came together to paint a historic picture. Looked at through the lens of history, those trenches, those drills, and those huts take on a very different meaning than they do out of context.

Of course, what helped those suffering through the winter of 1777–78 to soldier on and perform those menial tasks—to paint those individual brush strokes, one after another, day after day—was their understanding that their efforts belonged to a larger context. They may not have been able to predict the outcome of the war or to see at that time what impact the freedom they were fighting for would have on the world, but they knew they weren't just digging trenches and building huts so they could have trenches and huts: They were contributing to something much larger than themselves.

The Power of Perspective

Seeing the big picture means seeing . . . well, pretty much anything there is to see that relates to whatever it is you're looking at. In the case of *Irises*, seeing the big picture means seeing not only the brush strokes and the canvas, but also the frame, the gallery wall, the museum, the other visitors in the museum, the asylum in Saint-Rémy, the life of van Gogh, the impressionist movement, and the history of art, as well as where all of that fits in the context of history, culture, and society.

It's an awful lot to look at. In fact, it sounds kind of like quite a lot of effort. So why bother? What's to be gained from seeing this so-called big picture?

In a word, **perspective**.

Most often, we see an event or a situation at one level. Seeing things at only one level means, by definition, that we're getting a limited view of it—we're not seeing everything there is to see, which means we might be missing out on valuable information that could help us better or more fully understand what we're seeing. Gaining perspective is about stepping back or stepping forward so we can see at more than one level. The immediate benefit is the clearer understanding and deeper appreciation that comes from seeing a more complete and more accurate picture.

It's easy to hear "perspective" and assume it means taking a step back. But as we saw with my experience with *Irises*, I came to the museum already seeing the painting at the Canvas Level and the Context Level. What I saw taking a step forward and seeing at the Brush-Stroke Level was what I needed to see to complete the picture and fully appreciate what I had only partially understood before.

Often in class, we'll discuss a topic by starting with an abstract concept. Many times, what we need before we can fully understand this concept is the perspective that comes from stepping forward and seeing the issue at a closer level. For example, earlier we discussed the Crossroads Principle, which talks about the choices we make when we come to the major intersections along our path. That explanation is a Context-Level view. If I had left it at that level, some of you would have understood the principle, but some of you would not, and I'll bet most of you wouldn't have remembered it much beyond that page, let alone up until now. But I gave you the example of Rosa Parks, which helped you see the Crossroads Principle at the Brush-Stroke Level. We also discussed how her now-famous actions on the bus that day fit into the larger canvas of the civil rights movement. Seeing the principle at those closer, more concrete levels not only made it more clear and understandable, it also made it more memorable.

Clarity, understanding, and the appreciation they bring are not the only benefits of applying the Big Picture Approach. Gaining perspective also can prove valuable in four situations we all face often:

- Making decisions

- Solving problems

- Setting priorities

- Getting motivated

Let's take a closer look at all four.

Making Decisions in the Big Picture

Every day we're faced with dozens of decisions. Some are small: What should I have for lunch? How long should I study for history class? Where should I study? When should I go to bed?

Others are big: What major should I declare? Which French class should I take next semester? Should I get involved in that campus organization? What do I want to do this summer?

The Big Picture Approach can help us make better decisions, no matter what the question, because perspective gives us more information and more points of view and lets us take a greater context into account when we make those decisions.

For example, let's look at a couple of the previous questions. We'll start with a simple one: *What should I have for lunch?* If you're looking at the situation only from the Brush-Stroke Level, you might answer, "Whatever looks good at the cafeteria!" But take a step back first. What might be the drawback to such a limited perspective? Well, perhaps what looks good is a heavy, starchy entrée. If you choose that, will you find yourself falling asleep from food coma in your important afternoon class and missing out on valuable information? Taking a Canvas-Level approach, you might think about the last time you had that heavy meal and opt for something lighter, so you can be sharper in class in an hour.

Is there a Context-Level view to something as simple as your lunch decision? You bet. Maybe what looks good at the cafeteria isn't very healthy. If you choose to eat it today, you may not feel any ill effects. But if you make your lunch decision every day at the Brush-Stroke Level only, you increase the chances that you'll keep choosing unhealthy lunches (after all, the food that's bad for us usually is the food that looks most appetizing) and put your long-term health at risk. And what if whatever looks good is also the most expensive item on the menu? Brush-Stroke thinking day after day might mean you disregard the context of your meal plan or the money in your budget and find yourself coming up short at the end of the term—because of a series of short-sighted decisions you made weeks, or months, earlier.

I certainly don't want to discredit seeing things at the Brush-Stroke Level. Some days, you just need to eat the pepperoni pizza. We've all been there. But when you step back and gain perspective, you can see that it's not such a great idea to eat it every day.

Now how about one of those big-decision questions: *Should I get involved in that campus organization?* That seems like a simple enough decision on the surface. Am I interested in the group's activities? Do I like the people? Will I have a good time? In many cases, a positive answer to those questions is enough to get you to sign up. Sometimes, it takes even less—do you know people who have gotten involved with a campus organization because a bunch of their friends were doing it? Have you ever done that yourself?

It's not wrong for your friends to be your criteria for joining a campus organization—plenty of people discover things they're passionate about that way and find new friends in the bargain. But if you join every campus organization your friends join, or every one that interests you or sounds like fun, you might soon find you don't have any time left for your studies. So while the Brush-Stroke view might be fine on occasion, broadening your perspective to a Canvas view will help you make better decisions because, at that level, you'll ask better questions, such as: What is the time commitment for this organization? Do I value participating in it more than I value participating in other organizations? If I say "yes" to this organization, am I saying "no" to something else? If so, what? And if so, am I comfortable with that trade-off?

At an even larger, Context Level, you might ask different questions: Will participating in this organization help me advance toward my career goals? Can I gain valuable life experiences from my involvement? Will I be proud to put this campus group on my resume? Does participating in this organization fit into my Life Wedge?

Your Life Wedge is an excellent reference point in this decision-making process because it helps define the larger context of what's important to you, in terms of your dreams and your values. When you come to the crossroads of a big decision, the more information you have—the greater your perspective, and the bigger the picture in which you see that decision—the more confidently you can decide.

Journal Entry: Adding Perspective to Decision Making

In your journal, consider two questions you might face on a daily basis. Using the examples above as a guide, pick one small decision and one bigger decision that are relevant to your life. Then, for each decision, write down how that decision looks at the Brush-Stroke Level, the Canvas Level, and the Context Level. Write down questions you could ask yourself at each of those levels that might broaden your perspective, help you consider more information, and support sound decision making.

Perspective and Problem Solving

Have you ever heard someone ask for the "ten-thousand-foot view" of a situation? If so, you've heard someone asking for a different perspective. This phrase refers to an airplane in flight, with the idea being that once the plane has gotten up to that height, you're far enough from the ground that you're not worried about the details at the surface because you simply can't see them anymore— but you can see entire cities all at once. In other words, you can see things at a sort of macro–Context Level. From this height, you can get a systems-level view of the problem.

Think about a traffic jam. If you're stuck bumper-to-bumper, and no one ahead of you or behind you seems to be moving, you're unlikely to understand why because you're trapped at the Brush-Stroke Level. All you can see are the cars immediately surrounding you. There's definitely a problem, but you only understand its impact on you, not what's causing it, and from behind the wheel, you're in no position to solve it. All you can do is suffer from it and search for a traffic report on the radio.

If you're in the same situation and you're driving an 18-wheeler, your elevated cab likely has you sitting higher than the rest of the cars, so you may be able to see far enough ahead to understand the extent of the traffic jam. Maybe you can see how far ahead cars are stopped or possibly the actual cause of the problem.

You've got a Canvas-Level view, but again, there's little you can do about it. You're still stuck in the gridlock, and, most likely, you still don't have enough information to offer a solution.

But if you were in a traffic helicopter, you could rise high enough to see where the traffic jam begins and ends, see which roads are affected, and identify the cause of the jam. Your perspective would probably enable you to do this quickly and easily, and with that perspective and the additional information it provides, you'd be in a better position than the car or truck to solve the problem—you could get on the radio and contact the police or emergency services to tell them the exact source of the problem, you could call the radio station that gives the local traffic report to help them redirect traffic, or perhaps you could even land the chopper and lend a hand yourself. Regardless of your action, the broader perspective helps you solve the problem.

We face similar situations in our daily lives. In many cases, our initial perspective limits our ability to identify or execute the best solution to a problem. That initial perspective is our **access point**, the angle or perspective at which we first approach a situation.

For our own problems, our access point is usually the Brush-Stroke Level. This perspective makes sense—after all, we dip our brushes in the oil paint and put the brush strokes on the canvas every day; we know intimately the basic, boring details that we need to make it through each day, like which drawer we can find our socks in, which classroom to go to for our first class of the day, the shortest walking path to that building, and so forth. We paint dozens of brush strokes on a daily basis that even our best friend might not know about—because she's focused on her daily brush strokes, too.

However, as we saw with *Irises*, when you're close enough to see the brush strokes, you can miss the bigger picture. Whether we realize this consciously or sense it unconsciously, we usually understand the limitations of that access point, which is why we turn to friends and family when faced with a challenging problem; not only can they offer comfort and support, but they also can offer another perspective. Friends will have a different access point to the situation, usually a Canvas-Level view, which enables them to see things about our situation that we cannot. This view makes sense because they observe our lives from the outside and not from the inside, like we do. Often, a friend has just enough outside perspective to either spot the problem more clearly than we can, which can help us solve it, or ask insightful questions that lead toward a solution.

Why is it so often easier to understand (and sometimes solve) someone else's problem than it is our own? Because we're not so close to the other person's problem. When we're not the ones applying the paint—when we're looking over the painter's shoulder, so to speak—we see the whole canvas. We're not worried about the next dollop of paint; we're interested in what the picture as a whole looks like.

As you probably know from firsthand experience, a shift in perspective can be the first step in helping solve just about any kind of problem—personal, academic, organizational, and more. The benefits of taking that step back, of seeing things through the eyes of another, apply in almost every situation.

Sometimes, however, we need a broader perspective than even the Canvas-Level view to solve the problem. In these cases, we can turn to someone who can provide a Context-Level view, such as a professor, an advisor, or a mentor. These individuals may look at our specific problem from an even greater distance, but they usually have more experience with problems and situations generally; they can place what we're facing in a larger context and use deductive thinking to offer general suggestions that might help us solve our specific problem.

Journal Entry: With a Little Help from My Friends

Think of a time when you have asked someone else for help with a problem. In your journal, answer the following questions about the situation.

- What was the problem? Why do you think you were stuck?

- Whom did you turn to for help? What did you expect that person to offer you?

- How did that person help? What problem-solving strategies did he or she use?

- What can you take from the help that person provided that could help you solve your own problems in the future?

- Could what you learned from that person help you solve someone else's problem in the future? How?

Access Points and Academics

We know how a Canvas-Level view can help solve personal problems, but now let's take a look at access points in an academic setting and how a shift in perspective can help us in the classroom.

For most things outside of our own life, our access point is the Canvas Level. For example, that was our starting point with both van Gogh and Valley Forge. This is a logical and easy access point for us as outside observers. As we get more interested, we look more closely and examine things at the Brush-Stroke Level, where we see the specifics that contributed to the broader view. As we become curious about how this painting (literally, in the case of van Gogh, but metaphorically in the case of Valley Forge) fits in with other knowledge, with other social and cultural movements, we take a step back to learn more and appreciate what we're seeing at the Context Level.

Your access point is impacted by more than how close you are to a topic or situation, however. Your access point is also determined by the **lens** through which you look at the world. For example, if you're looking at *Irises* through the lens of an artist, you'll notice technique, color choices, and other things important to an artist. However, if you look at *Irises* through the lens of an art historian, you might think about the painting in the context of van Gogh's life or the impressionist movement. If you look at *Irises* through the lens of a psychologist, the painting may prompt you to think about van Gogh's mental state or about art therapy. And if you look at *Irises* through the lens of an economist, you might think about how the price of the painting at auction reflected larger economic trends at the time of the sale. Everybody is looking at the same painting, but they're not seeing the same thing.

No matter what you see in the world, there are many angles to consider—many viewpoints from which you might understand an idea, an event, or a problem. One of the great benefits of general education programs is that they expose us to many viewpoints different from our own through required classes in various subjects. As we take courses in sociology, psychology, history, fine arts, philosophy, religion, political science, literature, and more, we learn to see things through those lenses, which helps us better understand different angles or facets of our encounters.

The General Education Matrix on the next page looks at one particular subject—the civil rights movement, which we have discussed in this book—through the lenses of several fields commonly studied in general education programs. Take a few moments now to complete the exercise in the matrix.

In the following activity chart, look at the angle or perspective your professor and/or textbook in these classes may have taken.

1. Choose a topic that interests you and place it at the top of the third column. This topic can be a cause, development, or movement that you have discussed in one of your classes or something of your own choosing. A few examples include the Iraq war, global warming, technology, and health care.

2. Choose at least three of your general education classes from column one, and comment in column three on the angle of your topic that was taken, or one that could be taken, in that respective class.

Perhaps the best illustration of how valuable it can be to look at a problem or subject from multiple perspectives and through multiple lenses is to look at what happens when you approach something from only one perspective and one access point. Read the story of "The Blind Men and the Elephant" in the activity box on page 120 for an extreme example about the hazards of limited perspective.

Setting Priorities in Perspective

No matter what you do in your life, you have limits—limited time, limited resources, limited energy. I don't mean to suggest that there's anything you can't do if, as the saying goes, you put your mind to it. But I've learned that while you can do just about *anything* you want to do in life, you can't do *everything*. In other words, you need to set priorities.

Priorities are decisions you make about how and when to spend those limited resources. As with our discussion about decision making, the decisions

6.1 General Education Matrix

General Education Class	Angle in Looking at the Civil Rights Movement	Angle in Looking at a Cause (Development) of Your Choosing: _____
Sociology	The Jim Crow laws of the South created considerable tension between the races.	
Psychology	Daily oppression created personal issues related to self-worth and injustice.	
History	Various trials, laws, riots, and key personalities constituted the movement.	
Fine Arts	What do musical lyrics such as southern gospel and jazz tell us about southern culture? What about the paintings and sketches from that time?	
Philosophy	Was there a fatalistic or optimistic view of the world—would good triumph?	
Religion	The movement was closely linked with the southern Protestant churches—why? Also, why did Islam rise among the revolutionary sect?	
Political Science	The events of the movement had direct influences on the national elections.	
Literature	What works influenced the civil rights leaders? Was there a common theme? A common reading?	

you make to prioritize one thing over another can deal with small issues (I only have enough quarters for one load of laundry—should I wash a load of whites first, or a load of darks?) or big issues (I've been accepted for an internship this summer, and also for a study-abroad program, and I can't do both—which is more important to me?).

Whether you've given it much thought or not, you set priorities all the time. For example, if you decide to work on your English paper today because it's due tomorrow, and you put off your philosophy paper until later in the week, you've prioritized the English paper: you've chosen to place it ahead of other projects in terms of how you will invest your time and energy. But is being ruled by external constraints the best strategy for setting priorities?

We often set our priorities at the Brush-Stroke Level: We look at what has to happen today and put that first on our agenda. However, that approach often creates situations in which something that is urgent gets more of our attention, time, and energy than something that is important. Of course, if you really do have an English paper due tomorrow, I recommend that you work on it today. But once that's done, then what? Do you just wait for the next deadline to creep up on you and then go into urgent mode again? For many students,

6.2 Blind Men Elephant

The following is a well-known poem by John Godfrey Saxe (1816–1887) that is often cited in discussions about perspective, with a common moral being that "perspective makes all the difference." Or, to use his analogy more directly, sometimes our limited perspective is correct, but we still need more information to understand fully the bigger picture.

It was six men of Indostan
To learning much inclined,
Who went to see the Elephant
(Though all of them were blind),
That each by observation
Might satisfy his mind

The First approached the Elephant,
And happening to fall
Against his broad and sturdy side,
At once began to bawl:
"God bless me! but the Elephant
Is very like a wall!"

The Second, feeling of the tusk,
Cried, "Ho! what have we here
So very round and smooth and sharp?
To me 'tis mighty clear
This wonder of an Elephant
Is very like a spear!"

The Third approached the animal,
And happening to take
The squirming trunk within his hands,
Thus boldly up and spake:
"I see," quoth he, "the Elephant
Is very like a snake!"

The Fourth reached out an eager hand,
And felt about the knee.
"What most this wondrous beast is like
Is mighty plain," quoth he;
"'Tis clear enough the Elephant
Is very like a tree!"

(Continued)

6.2   **Blind Men Elephant** (Concluded)

The Fifth, who chanced to touch the ear,
Said: "E'en the blindest man
Can tell what this resembles most;
Deny the fact who can
This marvel of an Elephant
Is very like a fan!"

The Sixth no sooner had begun
About the beast to grope,
Than, seizing on the swinging tail
That fell within his scope,
"I see," quoth he, "the Elephant
Is very like a rope!"

And so these men of Indostan
Disputed loud and long,
Each in his own opinion
Exceeding stiff and strong,
Though each was partly in the right,
And all were in the wrong!

Moral:

So oft in theologic wars,
The disputants, I ween,
Rail on in utter ignorance
Of what each other mean,
And prate about an Elephant
Not one of them has seen!

that describes their semester—periods of frantic urgency and intense effort, interspersed with brief lulls in which no assignments are due and no work seems pressing.

Besides being an incredibly stressful way to live your life as a student, this approach limits your ability to succeed. That's because it's driven by a very narrow perspective on priorities.

Early in this book, you created a Life Wedge for yourself. I hope that with each passing chapter you have reconsidered your Life Wedge based on new information and have refined it so that it can be even more accurate and useful to you. Your Life Wedge can serve as a powerful tool for setting priorities as well. To use it that way, though, you have to take a step back from the perspective of today and see things in the big picture.

If all you see is today, for instance, then it's easy to understand why you would focus all of today's energies on tomorrow's deadline: You're faced with immediate consequences. It's like when you realize the night before a big interview that all of your dress clothes are in the dirty laundry pile. You're faced with consequences—either you take time the night before the interview to wash, dry, fold, and iron your laundry (assuming you have enough quarters), or you wear dirty clothes to the interview. Either way, a Brush-Stroke view can get you into that kind of situation.

But if you take a step back and see the larger canvas, you can make better decisions, as we discussed above, and you can set better priorities.

For example, let's say the deadline for that English paper isn't quite so pressing—it's not due tomorrow but rather in three days. And two days after that, your philosophy paper is due. That means that you have three days to work on the English paper and five to work on the philosophy paper. (I'm going to assume, perhaps generously, that you've already done the research and reading for both, and now you simply need to do the writing.) If you prioritize simply from the immediate view of the Brush-Stroke perspective, you will put all your energies and time into the English paper first because that's due first, and then when you've finished that, you'll focus on the philosophy paper.

But what if the philosophy paper counts for a larger percentage of your grade in that class than the English paper does? And what if you got a C on the last philosophy paper but a B on the last English paper? What if you've been struggling more with the concepts in your philosophy class, but you feel confident of your grasp of the subjects you've been discussing in English class? Putting off your philosophy paper until after you've finished your English paper makes less sense now, doesn't it? But until you take a step back for a bigger-picture view, you can't see that—you'll only see the deadlines that are staring you in the face. When you use the Big Picture Approach, however, you can see the benefit of balancing your priorities—in this case, investing some time in that philosophy paper *before* you've completed the English paper, even though the English paper is due first.

Remember the story about Tad, the "drummer," from Chapter 1? His story is a classic example of misplaced priorities. Although he said he wanted to be a drummer, he had sold his drum kit and bought a new car. He took a narrow perspective that prioritized the short-term benefits of a nice car over the long-term benefits of a drum set on which he could, you know, actually practice playing the drums. As a result, his career in music never materialized.

The broader and wider your perspective, the more effectively you can set smart, productive priorities about how to spend time, energy, money, or any precious resource. Once again, your Life Wedge serves as a helpful guide. By including it in your perspective, as with the decision-making process we discussed previously, you can define your priorities in the larger context of what's really important to you (your goals, values, and life purpose) and be more thoughtful and informed when you set them.

Journal Entry: Perspective and Priorities

Intentionally or not, you've set priorities for how to spend your time and resources this week. Look back at the last seven days, and in your journal, answer the following questions about the priority-setting process you used and ways you might set priorities differently in the future.

- What tasks did you prioritize this past week?

- Is your response based on time spent? The tasks you did first?

- Was this an intentional process of setting priorities, or did you just do it "on the fly"? Either way, looking back, was this an effective process?

- Did something not get done in the past week that you wanted to get done but did not make a priority? If so, what? What do you think happened?

- What could you do to set priorities more purposefully for the coming week?

- What perspectives would you need to take into account to set priorities more effectively? What questions could you ask yourself?

A New Perspective on Motivation

How motivated would you be if I handed you a shovel and asked you to dig a trench?

It's okay—I understand if your motivation would be low. Ditch-digging is hard, sweaty, dull work. There's no glamour in it. There's no glory. There's usually little reward, unless you find calluses and a sore back rewarding.

But what if it were the winter of 1777–78, and we were at Valley Forge, and I explained how vitally important it was for the safety of our encampment that we have several miles of adequate trenches dug, and I handed you a shovel . . . would you be more motivated to dig a trench then?

Of course you would; trench-digging would no longer be an abstract, laborious task. In that broader context, you would see that it served a greater purpose, specifically, your short-term survival and, more generally, the cause of freedom for a new nation. Because of the perspective you gained by applying the Big Picture Approach, you could likely find the motivation to do a dreary task that in another context might not motivate you at all. I bet you'd even be motivated to dig the highest-quality trench that you could, and dig it with enthusiasm. You'd still get those calluses, of course, but you'd probably feel differently about them as well. You might even show them off to your friends.

This is perhaps the greatest power of perspective: the power to motivate. Here again, your Life Wedge plays a critical role. It's kind of like a Context-Level motivation power tool. Let me explain what I mean by that. In defining your Ideal Wedge, you focused on big picture things: dreams, goals, careers, and values. When faced with a task that you're not immediately motivated to complete (like digging a trench, for example), take a step back and broaden your perspective to the Context Level. With this wider view, you can determine whether that task is linked in any way to the larger goals addressed in your Life Wedge. If it is connected, you may find it easier to motivate yourself to buck up and do the task. If it's not connected in any way, then it's fair to question whether the task is worth doing.

In some cases, you may have to think creatively, or *really* Big Picture, to find the connection—after all, it's not exactly a *short* line between digging trenches in January and achieving independence from Great Britain—but with a Big Picture view, you can see all the dots between the two, and realize that if you're going to connect them, it may start with digging that trench.

A word to the wise here: It helps to think these things through before the difficult task is staring you in the face. Let's say, for example, that you've included physical health in your Life Wedge. You want to be healthy, happy, and vital for many years, enough to chase your grandchildren around the playground. Well, that's quite an abstract vision, considering that scene in your head might not take place for 30 years or so. But decisions you make today do influence whether or not that dream will come true: decisions like whether to walk to class or take the campus shuttle; decisions like whether to head to the athletic complex for an hour before dinner or hang out in the dorm and kill time talking to your friends or playing video games; decisions like whether to eat a healthy snack when the hunger pang hits mid-afternoon or just grab a candy bar from the vending machine.

In each of those pairs of tasks, motivation is needed to choose (and act on) the former option over the latter. When we choose the latter, even though we know we should choose the former, we usually do so because those latter decisions are simply easier in the moment. I hope by now you can see how in-the-moment thinking can be a recipe for trouble if that's the only kind of thinking you do. If you think about those three scenarios before they happen, however, you can avoid having to make an in-the-moment decision, and you can take time to consider how those choices connect to the goals in your Life Wedge. More important, you can think about ways to make it easier to make the choice you've said you want to make. For example, maybe you set your alarm 10 minutes earlier in the morning to give yourself more time to walk to class, and maybe you also arrange to meet a friend so you can walk together. Now you have more time and a new motivation—you want to meet your friend to walk and talk together. Suddenly, it's easier to make that choice; it's easier to summon the motivation. But you have to get beyond the "right-here, right-now" perspective to get to that point. The same goes with the other motivation dilemmas. What if you didn't go back to the dorm after class, but instead decided in advance to go straight to the athletic complex to work out, and you made sure you had your workout clothes waiting for you in the locker room? What if you knew you always got hungry around mid-afternoon, and over the weekend got some baby carrots and some apples that you could keep in your backpack for when the snack attack hits?

If you take the Big Picture Approach, you can plan ahead and make it easier to be motivated. Make no mistake; motivation and willpower are critically important for success, but they're also energy intensive. Only people who are completely stuck at the Brush-Stroke Level will keep putting themselves in situations that demand the kind of energy needed for superior motivation and willpower all the time.

What about when a situation doesn't call for an either/or choice but rather a decision of degree? For example, let's say you have a biology test coming up in a few weeks. You're going to study for it—that's not really the question. The question is, how will you study for it? Will you put in a 100-percent studying effort? If so, what does that look like? Does it mean creating flash cards weeks in advance, reviewing your notes once a week, reviewing the flash cards for 20 minutes a day, rereading the chapters? To put in a 100-percent effort would be to do everything you could possibly do to assure your best performance on the test. Certainly you're capable of putting in that kind of effort. But are you motivated to put in 100 percent? Or are you only motivated to put in 80 percent? If so, why? Is it because an 80-percent effort is simply less taxing, or because you're not motivated to excel in biology?

I often see students who put in an 80-percent effort not because they've thought through their priorities or thought about their Life Wedge and connected the dots between studying and their long-term goals, but because 80-percent effort simply isn't that difficult to muster. They've learned they can get by with an 80-percent effort, and looking at things at the Brush-Stroke Level, they're not sure it's worth it to work harder to increase their effort to 90 percent or 100 percent.

This is a dangerous trap. I understand the thinking behind it, and I realize you can't put forth a 100-percent effort for every assignment in every class. We talked in the last section about setting priorities, determining what's most important to you in the big picture, and directing your best efforts toward that. This is different. What I'm talking about here is defining your best effort, making intentional decisions about the activities and tasks that deserve your best effort, and connecting those activities to your Life Wedge to help you summon the motivation to invest a 100-percent effort in the things that you've decided matter most.

Only you can know if you're investing enough effort to meet your goals. My challenge to you is to use the power of perspective to help motivate you to invest the right effort in the right tasks at the right time.

Journal Entry: What's Your Big-Picture Motivation?

In your journal, take a few moments to reflect on the things that motivate you. The following questions can serve as prompts to get you started:

- What is something you know you should do but often can't find the motivation to do? Applying a larger perspective, how can you connect this activity to something in your Life Wedge? How does that connection impact your motivation?

- What is something you find it easy to get motivated to do that others might not find so easy? Why do you think you are so motivated for this task? Do you see a direct connection between this activity and a bigger-picture goal? If so, what is it?

- Think of a situation in which you've given a 100-percent effort. What did that effort look like? Why do you think you were motivated to give that kind of effort? What lessons can you take from that experience to apply to other situations in your life?

Applying the Big Picture Approach

Now that you understand the value of applying the Big Picture Approach, how can you apply it? The following guidelines will help you apply the Big Picture Approach to many life situations, including your academic efforts, your relationships, and your college experience in general:

1. *Take a step back (or forward).* Are you feeling the elephant's tail and concluding that the elephant is like a rope? If you think you might be too close to the problem or situation, take a step back. If that doesn't give you the clarity and perspective you need to make your decision, solve the problem, set your priorities, find the motivation, or simply understand what you're seeing accurately, perhaps you were too far away to begin with, and a step forward is what you need. The key is to shift your focus. Just remember that you may have to adjust it a few times to get the right perspective.

2. *See beyond your here and now.* Sometimes to see the big picture, you need to leave your familiar surroundings entirely. I'm reminded here of the story of Gautama Buddha. His father, the king of the Shakya nation (near modern-day Nepal) around 500 B.C., had protected him from the common people throughout his life. At age 29 years, Gautama left the palace grounds and began touring the nearby town, where he saw for the first time the sick and infirm. This shift in perspective became a crossroads experience for him—he would eventually leave behind his elite upbringing and become a monk, looking for a way to help all people, rich and poor, find happiness. In your life, you might apply the Big Picture Approach by making choices that take you outside of your comfort zone, like participating in a service project that helps people who are very different from you or taking a class in a new, challenging subject.

3. *Find your reference points.* When I think of the Big Picture Approach, I'm reminded of my childhood days on the farm when I was sent out to plow the fields. The key to plowing correctly is to plow in a straight line, and the key to plowing in a straight line is finding reference points to anchor you. Often these were fence posts or distant trees, and fixing my eyes on them would help me to plow straight. I apply the same principle when I'm navigating large cities. In Chicago, I look for the John Hancock Center—it's an obvious reference point that orients me in space and helps me get my bearings. In St. Louis my reference point is the Gateway Arch; in Indianapolis, it's Monument Circle. (For those on the East or West Coast, please forgive my Midwestern references; I'm a Midwestern boy at heart.) Your reference point may be something concrete, like a monument or landmark, or something you read to remind yourself of what's important and help you get your bearings, like your Life Wedge diagram, your personal mission statement, or a quote or book that is especially meaningful to you. People also can serve as reference points. Many of us turn to a

parent, friend, advisor, or mentor for wisdom and insight. These reference points can give us perspective and help remind us of what's important and where we're supposed to be going.

4. *Connect what you see with what you know.* By broadening our view, the Big Picture Approach can help us link what we learn to an experience, which helps us understand what we learn more fully. This experience can be something we've lived firsthand or something we've observed (either real or fictional). I recently encountered a student asking about the "unused" food from our student center café. Although she asked tactfully, and in a way that most people would not identify as out of desperation, I saw before me a scene from 30 years earlier, when my roommate and I had $9 total between us to survive for two weeks. Recalling that incident, and connecting my experience with this student's experience, helped me empathize with her and motivated me to help. Whether in a personal or an academic situation, connecting what you see with something you know provides a frame of reference and can increase your understanding and ability to act.

5. *Put what you see in context.* Seeing the big picture—looking at things at the Context Level—can help you identify causes and motivations for actions and decisions that might simply escape your comprehension at the Brush-Stroke or Canvas Level. One of the best questions you can ask of any conclusion or any new information is, "So what?" By linking small bits of information to larger ones, you can begin to see their relevance. An example of this is the Rosa Parks story. If you knew about the incident on the bus but only knew about her daily frustrations, the incident might make sense but not seem significant. However, placing this incident in the larger context of the Jim Crow laws and the daily reliance of workers on bus transportation begins to paint a fuller picture. And when these events are further connected to the broader movement of civil rights activities, Parks's boldness that day and the ensuing arrest take on heightened importance. Out of context, Rosa Parks was just a woman who refused to give up her seat on a bus. In context, she was, as Congress called her, the "Mother of the Modern-Day Civil Rights Movement."

6. *Choose your brush strokes wisely.* While the Big Picture Approach enables us to see, think, and plan at the Context Level and the Canvas Level, ultimately, we can only act at the Brush-Stroke Level. As a result, the brush strokes we paint each day matter, for they are the building blocks of our present and our future. Taking a Big Picture Approach enables us to have the perspective, context, information, and understanding to choose those brush strokes wisely.

Chapter 6 Review

SUMMARY OF MAJOR CONCEPTS

- The broader our perspective of something, the more clearly we can understand it and the more productively we can interact with it.

- We generally come at information or a situation from one perspective, also known as an access point.

- If we understand the limitations of our access point, we can step forward or step back to add perspective and see a bigger picture, which will help us understand what we're seeing more clearly.

- Taking a Big Picture Approach can help us make decisions, solve problems, and set priorities by placing them in a larger context.

- When learning about an academic subject, the Big Picture Approach can help by putting a face on a general idea or placing a specific incident or experience in a broader context.

- Our daily actions, or brush strokes, have an impact on the big picture of both our present and our future.

KEY TERMS

Brush-Stroke Level   the up-close view of something. At this level, you are close enough to see fine levels of detail.

Canvas Level   a view that is a bit farther back than the Brush-Stroke Level. At this level, you can see a fuller picture than you can at the closer Brush-Stroke Level.

Context Level   a view that enables you not only to see a full picture of the thing or situation at which you're looking but also to place it in a larger context.

Big Picture Approach   a philosophy that encourages taking a broad view. This approach includes seeing things at the Brush-Stroke, Canvas, and Context Levels.

perspective   literally, a point of view; in our discussions, it refers to seeing something at a different distance or from a different angle.

access point   the view, angle, or perspective at which you first interact with a person, situation, or piece of information.

lens   the perspective you hold that is determined by your personal circumstances or experiences such as your job, academic specialization, or cultural background.

APPLICATION EXERCISE

Worst-Case Scenario

In this chapter, we've discussed the benefits of a broad perspective and of using the Big Picture Approach. In this exercise, let's take a look at what happens if we only take a small-picture approach and operate from a limited perspective.

In the left column of the matrix below are listed several aspects of your college experience. In the middle column, pick one level at which to view that aspect—Brush-Stroke Level, Canvas Level, or Context Level. Then, in the third column, write down what would happen if you *only* addressed that aspect of your college experience from that level. Think about the limitations you might encounter from only looking at things from that one perspective and how they might affect your ability to succeed.

Aspect of Your College Experience	Level for Viewing This Aspect (Brush Stroke, Canvas, or Context)	Consequences of Only Viewing This Aspect at This Level
Choosing classes		
Participating in campus organizations		
Planning a study schedule		
Socializing		
Eating		
Sleeping		
Reading Assigned Books		

REMINDER

The Wedge Principle is built around events familiar to us. As we look again at our Wedge diagrams, we should ask how many of our goals and decisions came from interacting with the same reference points as others have. The interesting aspect is that some of these same events had radically different results in the lives of others. Can you think of such examples? Did you sit through a class or lecture you loved, that made you think about your Life Wedge, and yet a peer or peers seemed unmoved?

3 A Purpose-Guided Plan

A graduation ritual celebrates the heights to which an education can take a person.

The Sock at Graduation

My college roommate strutted onto the graduation platform, lanky arms raised, soaking in the applause and begging for more. He didn't notice the crusty old tube sock pinned to his bottom.

This was the day he'd been waiting for, and he wasn't about to let any stuffy rules of graduation protocol ruin it: With a long stride, he stepped to the front of the stage and gave a lock-wristed wave worthy of a queen. Then he crouched, lowering his arms with his palms upward, and began begging the crowd for more noise—which they happily gave him. Although his four years had only earned him a two-year degree, and although his honors ribbon was borrowed from me, he had stolen the show.

Or so he thought.

The louder the crowd roared, the more he strutted, and the more obvious was the sock pinned to him like a tail on a donkey. With one last turn to face the crowd, he whipped the long sock around, nearly knocking the glasses off the face of one of the shocked dignitaries on the platform.

The sock in question was his, one of many he had piled in the corner of our room in a mountain of laundry that never seemed to get clean. He could afford to buy new clothes rather than wash the dirty ones, and so he did. This was my payback. But for those precious moments, he felt he had the world by the tail . . . until finally he realized he had one of his own.

In an instant, his smile became lifeless, and his eyes glared at me across the stage. Admitting defeat, he raised his long right arm and sheepishly pointed my way. The crowd went crazy again—it was a moment to cherish for us both. As popular as he was rich, and as good-natured as he was carefree, my lively roommate finally graduated.

Another memorable moment occurred more recently on the same graduation platform, though no dirty socks were involved. Instead of begging for applause with wild waves, a quiet young man passed almost unnoticed in front of the crowd. He followed the Parson triplets, and—triplets being a guaranteed crowd-pleaser at any commencement ceremony—the audience was still abuzz when the announcer paused and caught the eye of the next graduate before reading his name: "Jason David Tiller Pattengale." It was a young man whose first father was killed by a teenager and whose second dad writes this account.

Jason nearly missed his graduation ceremony—he had visited three surgeons in the previous four weeks; his Crohn's disease was taking its toll.

While other seniors crammed for their exams, he endured CAT scans.

While others worried about getting an "A," Jason was hooked to a *Remicade* bag four hours away.

While students watched *Survivor* and *Deal or No Deal*, he was surviving the realities of prednisone and after-effects that were all too real.

When he was bedridden and 30 pounds underweight, Crohn's disease was something we all began to hate. But though he often had to shuttle directly from doctors' offices to classroom exams, he stayed the course.

Although many times he had to crawl from his bed in the morning and endure days that began with a handful of pills before proceeding to classes and work, he often ended his days doing back flips in a distant city—because he was elected captain of his nationally ranked college cheer team for his senior year.

While his peers loaded up on Starbucks to get them through all-nighters, Jason learned to live without caffeine. He learned to order two bottom buns on his fast-food burgers to avoid sesame seeds and to pass on French fries, popcorn, nuts, and soda. He learned how to monitor his own iron levels and keep multiple prescriptions current. He lived for a while with a colostomy bag and, among several other surgeries, survived the removal of his entire colon.

Jason didn't graduate with honors, but he graduated on time, and he hardly needed to borrow my ribbon to be honorable—the very fact of his graduation was an honor in itself.

Along the way, Jason learned many valuable lessons, the foremost among them being this: *The dream must be stronger than the struggle.* His perseverance was a clear demonstration of his priorities.

He also learned that no matter what challenges or troubles you encounter, life goes on; healthy or not, the calendar still turns, friends progress, and bills accrue. He could have easily, and perhaps justifiably, backed away from the challenges of being a full-time college student and fighting Crohn's disease simultaneously. But he learned that life goes on, and he chose not to miss it.

As a professor, I marched in the recessional and noticed many other graduates there in spite of challenges—financial challenges, family challenges, personal challenges. I suspect that for each of them, as for my family, those challenges only served to make the accomplishment more sweet. Reaching dreams despite challenges touches the human spirit. Those diplomas are exclamation points highlighting important sentences in compelling life stories.

Whether rich or poor, outgoing or shy, healthy or challenged, the path to a diploma is a privileged preparation for life. Whether you're the valedictorian like Jason's roommate, a wealthy jokester like my old roomie, or a challenged student with a remarkable will, when you walk that platform, you are all called by the same name: graduate.

When Jason and his fellow graduates go out in the world to pursue careers—indeed, as you too will soon go out into the world—most employers see the degree and the GPA, not the journey that was taken to earn them. But for those doing the earning, and those who support them along the way, it's the journey that gives the degree its true potency.

AUTHOR'S COMMENTS

Some of you may feel more resonance with my roommate's journey than my son's. Some of you have faced tremendous obstacles that seem much more serious than either the distraction of family pressure or physical limitations. Many of you will find yourself somewhere in between. My sincere hope is that sharing these stories helps you reflect on your own journey—to envision graduation and forge ahead.

I've seen the joy close-up in my son's face and from a bit further away as thousands of my students have walked the platform. Many of these students weathered serious breakups that nearly destroyed them and their degrees; some struggled to survive financially, while others fought depression, hyperactivity, sleep apnea, and a host of other frustrating challenges that affected them every day. Hundreds have lost grandparents, dozens have lost parents, and several have lost brothers or sisters while navigating college's challenging waters.

No matter how long or winding the path, everyone who appears on that graduation platform has overcome challenges, with the most common being motivation. Sustained motivation is the common thread, the common ingredient for success, in all of these stories.

QUESTIONS

1. Can you or someone you know relate to either of the journeys in the article?

2. Can you think of anything that realistically might keep you from graduating?

3. What is your greatest personal asset in reaching graduation?

4. Are you motivated to finish college? How do you know?

5. What do you hope to do immediately after graduation?

SOURCE: Adapted from the author's article in *The Chronicle Tribune* (Paxton Media), June 2006. Used here with permission.

7 Taking Ownership of Your Education

An Amateur Effort

Even if you consider yourself a golf fan, you've probably never heard of Mike Bell. The owner of a school-services company in Indianapolis, Mike hasn't won a dime as a golfer. His name doesn't come up in a search on Golf.com. Yet he's enjoyed a career in the sport that most golfers could only dream about.

While balancing the normal commitments of life, family, and his business career, Mike was mostly a recreational golfer throughout his younger years. He was a very *good* recreational golfer, and he practiced and played every week, but he could never dedicate as much time to developing his game as he would have liked.

When he turned 50, he set a goal for himself: to become the United States Golf Association (USGA) Senior Amateur Champion.

With more time to concentrate on golf, he explains, "I went and started practicing really, really hard. I never thought I would attain that goal, but you have to have goals. And when I went down to Florida and would practice in the wintertime, the guys would say to me, 'Man, why don't you come and play? Why do you practice all the time?'"

"I said, 'Well, I want to have a chance at being the Senior Amateur Champion.' And everybody thought I was crazy. But I kept getting better."

When he turned 55, Mike became eligible for the Senior Tour, and in 2006, at age 59, he had his best year ever, winning more tournaments that year than he'd won his whole life. But it didn't look like he'd have a shot at the Senior Amateur Championship: In the qualifying tournament, he struggled on the final hole and ended up as the first alternate.

Shortly after winning the Senior Amateur Championship of Indiana, just a week before the USGA Senior Amateur Championship, Mike found out that one of his fellow Hoosiers was bowing out of the tournament for personal reasons. Mike was no longer the first alternate: He was in.

Mike made the most of his opportunity, sinking an eight-foot putt for par on the 18th hole to win the title at Victoria National Golf Club in his home state of Indiana. "Outside of marrying my wife, this is the greatest day in my life," he said after winning the Frederick L. Dold Trophy as the 2006 USGA Senior Amateur Champion.

"I love this trophy. Can I keep it?"[1]

The STIC Method

Practice and skill are undoubtedly two major keys to Mike's success. But he also has a strategy he applies to the mental side of the game: the **STIC Method**. This method involves four distinct steps: stop, think, imagine, and commit. Mike explained that he goes through this sequence before every shot he takes.

First, he'll **stop** at his ball, blocking out distractions and focusing only on the shot at hand. Then he'll consult with his caddy and **think** through the yardage and the best approach to the hole. Next, he'll pull the right club out of the bag and stand behind the ball and **imagine** his shot—from the backstroke of the swing all the way through to the ball in flight. Depending on the shot, he may even picture it landing on the green and rolling toward the hole. Finally, he'll **commit** to his plan and take the shot.

Mike told me, "When you see golfers pull the club from the bag, they've committed." Occasionally, he explained, if something doesn't feel right, they'll walk away from the ball, start the process anew, and sometimes choose a different club. The routine is so habitual and ingrained that they recognize when they approach the ball whether they're in or out of focus, and if they feel out of focus or that they haven't actually committed, they'll take a step back and start the process over. He added that when a golfer struggles, it's usually from losing focus during the most basic tasks.

The STIC Method that Mike applies to golf can be applied to our lives as well. So often, we're in such a rush to get to the next thing, to take that next shot, that we don't focus, plan, or commit—we just plow forward. Using Mike's approach, we can stop to focus on what we're doing, think through what's in front of us and possible paths we might take, and imagine the outcomes that might result from our choices. Ultimately, we must commit to a path and live with the consequences. However, if we've applied a routine that requires reflection and planning, like the STIC Method, we improve our chances of choosing the right path and being pleased with the outcome.

Taking Charge of Routine Tasks

We all have routines in our lives: a morning ritual that carries us from bed to our first class, a bedtime ritual that brings the day to a close and puts us to sleep, and countless more in between that impact how we study, with whom we interact, and when and where we eat, among other things. The question is, have your routines become your routines by **default** or by **design**?

---

[1] 2006 USGA Senior Amateur, www.senioram.org/2006/index.html.

If you're just letting events come to you, and your daily habits have been formed unintentionally, then your routine has evolved by default. You haven't put much thought into it, either in determining the steps in your routine or in evaluating its usefulness or effectiveness. If you're repeating routines you've fallen into by default, you may be limiting your ability to get things done, to maximize your talent, and to succeed.

On the other hand, if you have thought through your habits and decided in advance what your routines will look like, what they're intended to accomplish, and how to determine their effectiveness, then you've developed your routines by design. You're in control, and that's where real personal power lies—*controlling the design and designing the control.*

My friend's brother Carl designed a routine while he was in college that involved studying four hours each day. Thinking about his mental energy and his study habits, he knew he could stay focused on schoolwork for up to four hours, but after that, he would be less effective. He also knew he had four hours in his schedule to devote to studying, sometimes scattered in chunks throughout the day, sometimes in concentrated blocks. For many of my friends and me, four hours a day sounded like way too much—or not enough. On an average day, when the big test was still days away, four hours seemed excessive. On the night before an exam, four hours didn't seem like nearly enough—we'd load up on caffeine, stay up all night, and drag ourselves into the classroom the next morning, bleary-eyed, to take the exam. But Carl always strolled into class calm, rested, even showered, because even the night before an exam, he only studied four hours.

The consistent, focused effort he applied through his very intentional studying routine paid off. He finished with a 4.0 G.P.A., and today, 30 years later, he's a successful insurance actuary and the chair of our college's Board of Trustees.

On the other hand, a group of my college classmates had a study routine that involved them heading to the local diner to "tank up" on coffee to get ready to study. But this ritual was more than caffeine loading—they would socialize until around 3:00 a.m., when they would finally begin looking through their notes for the first time. I joined them at the diner a few times (with my studies basically finished), and enjoyed laughing and hanging out for a couple of hours. I certainly didn't get much studying done on those nights, and it turns out several of the others in attendance didn't either: Two of the brightest students in the group soon found themselves on academic probation and barely finished college, while a few others from the group never did. As for me, I realized they were inviting me primarily so they could borrow my notes and that joining them for their alleged study time actually put my own grades in jeopardy.

Observing these examples, I saw how routines can work for you or against you. The key lesson here is to take responsibility for your routines and to control the design of them so that you can design control into your life.

Journal Entry: A Routine You Can STIC To

Take a few moments to consider some of the routines you employ on a regular basis. Do you have a morning ritual? An evening ritual? How did those evolve—by default or by design? Now let's think for a minute about your academic routines. In your journal, answer the following questions:

- What is the routine you currently go through when you receive a homework assignment?

- Is this routine effective? Why or why not?

- Is this a routine that has evolved by default, or is it one you have designed? If by design, what process did you use to develop the routine?

- Using the STIC acronym, sketch out a routine that would help you complete new assignments more effectively:

  Stop: _____

  Think: _____

  Imagine: _____

  Commit: _____

- In what other ways could the STIC Method help you in your daily tasks?

Taking Responsibility for Learning

For many 18-year-old students entering college straight from high school, college is a social experience more than an educational one. The excitement of a new place, new friends, new activities, new opportunities, and, for many people, living away from home for the first time, all grab more of their attention and focus than their coursework. For many returning and older students, and oftentimes transfer students, college is more about achievement than education. These students generally come to college with a specific academic objective and purpose and are often focused on checking off course requirements and completing their degree so that they can add it to their resume, get a new job, or get a raise.

However, I think a true educational experience is both social and academic, filled with play and achievement—and learning. There is so much to learn in the classroom that if you focus only on what's happening with friends or student organizations, you'll miss out on the rich learning opportunities that occur when thinkers (and, by that, I mean not just faculty but students too) gather together to discuss, dissect, challenge, and explore concepts and ideas. At the same time, if you come to campus like it's a job, and you clock in and clock out, focused only on the end product, you can miss out not only on the opportunity to engage with a community of thinkers, but also on the valuable, unscripted social experiences that take place outside the classroom, and from which there is also so much to learn.

I certainly do not want to downplay the value and importance of socializing and enjoying yourself, nor do I want to discount the prestige and credibility that come with a college degree. But when you've graduated, and the social activities are in the past and the diploma is on your wall, what will you have to show for your college experience? A collection of fun memories and a framed piece of paper? Or will you have grown into a wiser, more capable, and more mature person?

Few places in the world offer the opportunities and resources of a college campus. Here, you have freedom to explore and experiment on a daily basis. You're guaranteed to find like-minded people and people whose views couldn't be more different from yours, and you're in a setting where you can socialize with and learn from both. Passionate people committed to causes sit next to you in lectures and in the cafeteria or break room. And every classroom has a certified expert at the front of the room who is there to help you learn the subject to which he or she has devoted years of study.

Yet so many students, in focusing only on the social aspect or the achievement aspect, miss out on all of that. Even worse, I think many students assume that simply by being on a college campus, learning happens. They absolve themselves of responsibility for learning, pawning it off on the college. This never works. It simply doesn't happen that way because you are not an education customer—you are a student.

Your college can't sell you an education, or even give it to you. It can't grant you knowledge, or inject you with learning, or infuse you with wisdom. What your college can do, however, is provide the environment, the support, the curriculum, and the resources for you to learn. But you have to take responsibility for your learning—both inside and outside the classroom. This chapter is about what happens when you make the choice to take responsibility for learning—when you take ownership of your education.

Keep in mind that your college also has accepted responsibility—from its trustees, from your state, and from accrediting agencies—to provide that environment, support, curriculum, and resources and to work constantly to make them the best they can be. But the college needs you to be an equal partner in the relationship because without students, there is no education.

A Big Picture Approach to How We Learn

Taking responsibility for your learning can sound like an intimidating task if you only see it at the Context Level. But applying the Big Picture Approach, we can remember that while the Context and Canvas Level are necessary for perspective and understanding, our daily actions occur at the Brush-Stroke Level. That's also the level at which we execute our routines on a daily basis. To take responsibility for our learning effectively, we must first understand the big picture of our learning process so that we can then identify and design appropriate routines that we can use to help us reach our learning goals.

Key to understanding the learning process is understanding the different types of learning and the different ways we learn. Learning can be divided into three categories: **knowledge**, **skills**, and **dispositions** (commonly referred to as one's *outlook* or *attitude*).

These three types of learning represent a Big Picture Approach to education. Much as the three levels of the Big Picture Approach that we discussed in the last chapter are linked and interconnected, so too are these three types of learning intertwined. Colleges teach to all three aspects of learning because they don't simply want to produce people who can do well in a trivia contest or who mean well but lack the skill and knowledge to do well; they aim to graduate whole people—capable, well-rounded individuals who can apply their knowledge, skills, and dispositions to make a contribution to their communities and the world.

Let's take a closer look at these three facets of learning.

Knowledge

This aspect of learning is rather straightforward: just the facts. If you're studying to be a doctor, for example, there is a long list of subjects related to health and the body that need to be mastered. Within each of these subjects are hundreds of subsets of information that must be learned as well. Because standardized tests determine if graduates can continue into medicine, the value of learning this specific knowledge has direct impact on future plans.

Other disciplines have their own specialized knowledge that must be mastered to achieve success. In fine arts, the knowledge base includes lists of painters, sculptors, and composers. In history, it's important to know about key kings, queens, and political developments. If you have decided on a major, you should be able to determine the main subjects you'll be studying and the subsets of knowledge you will be expected to master. In some courses, tests are given at the beginning and the end of the term to assess the knowledge learned through that particular class.

Knowledge is the "what" of learning, and at the knowledge level, memorization—of facts, formulas, dates, names, and so forth—is a common learning method. Though knowledge may be the most simple and accessible level of learning, it is still valuable and important: Knowledge you have gained can help you make informed decisions, which, as we've discussed, are the building blocks for achieving your dreams.

An appreciation of the value of knowledge also can help direct your learning. It enables you to look at a subject or situation and identify what information you need to understand it fully, to consider what knowledge is needed for success in certain careers, and then to seek out that knowledge.

Skills

If knowledge is the "what" of learning, skills are the "how"—learning a skill is learning how to apply the knowledge you've gained throughout your lifetime. While knowledge is power, knowledge applied through skill is even more powerful.

Knowledge generally refers to a learned set of information; skills usually refer to mastery of techniques. This mastery also may be referred to as expertise, proficiency, or ability. The most common method for learning a skill is to be taught the skill by an experienced instructor, and then to practice and refine the skill yourself over time. Colleges develop their programs and curricula to teach students both basic skills, which are expected of any graduate, and specific skills that are expected of graduates of a particular major or career track.

The most common skill sets are **Academic**, **Communication**, and **Trade Skills**. Academic Skills generally consist of logic and critical reasoning, which we've discussed, and reading. Communication Skills fall into two prominent categories: interpersonal and group communication. Subsets of interpersonal communication skills include oral skills (speech, listening, and interacting with others in conversation), group skills (social dialogue, small group interaction, large group interaction, mass communication, etc.), and writing. The Trade Skills, sometimes referred to as "professional skills" or "skilled trades," include a variety of learned techniques, from managing stock portfolios to welding.

Using technology is a skill that is fast becoming a universitywide requirement—and it fits into all of the above categories. An online search of skills surveys or skills lists will return a wide variety of skill indexes addressed in learning settings. One that many students find useful is the skills search on the Occupational Information Network Web site at http://online.onetcenter .org/skills.

Dispositions

A disposition is "a tendency to exhibit frequently, consciously, and voluntarily a pattern of behavior directed to a broad goal."[2] Another way of defining a disposition might be that it is a mindset, outlook, or attitude that you bring to all the things you do. It is the "why" to the "what" of knowledge and the "how" of skills—a reason to use your knowledge and skills, and a tendency or inclination actually to put them to work.

For example, if you are a history major, the knowledge you learn might include facts about key figures, dates, battles, and so forth. The skills you learn would include how to interpret certain events, how to read documents critically, how to identify trends and compare or link events from different eras, and how to write about history. Your disposition toward history, however, is more personal. It could be your motivation for learning history, a specific outlook you bring to the subject, or a passion you have for sharing what you've learned with others through teaching or writing.

Dispositions can be more general as well. You could cultivate a disposition to be a lifelong learner, a better citizen, or a lover of humanitarian causes. While these might seem like mindsets that you either have or you don't, they can be taught and encouraged by your college. For example, if your school identifies lifelong learning as a desired disposition for its graduates, it could emphasize learning opportunities outside the classroom, and professors, encouraged to support lifelong learning by the school, could look to identify and promote

---

[2] Liliain G. Kantz, "Dispositions as Educational Goals." ERIC: ED363454 (1993).

curiosity and a joy for new ideas and concepts in their classes through their teaching style and their assignments.

Ron Ritchhart, an education scholar who specializes in learning environments, believes that dispositions are "acquired patterns of behavior that are under one's control and will."[3] In his book, *Intellectual Character: What It Is, Why It Matters, How to Get It*, he argues:

> Dispositions concern not only what we can do, our abilities, but what we are actually likely to do, addressing the gap we often notice between our abilities and our actions. . . . More than desire and will, dispositions must be coupled with requisite ability. Dispositions motivate, activate, and direct our abilities.

In other words, it is our disposition that turns ideas into actions and makes knowledge truly powerful. For example, plenty of Dr. Martin Luther King's contemporaries felt the same sting of injustice that he felt but kept silent or participated but did not lead. Dr. King had a disposition to act, not to accept injustice as inevitable, and so he led a movement that utilized a wide variety of knowledge and skills, from how to organize events and how to manage finances for a social movement to writing and diplomacy.

St. Norbert College (in De Pere, Wisconsin) provides a thoughtful and concise list of dispositions that it expects of its students who graduate with teaching degrees. Its list of "Pre-service Teacher Dispositions" states that teachers graduating from St. Norbert College will be "dedicated, principled, creative, proactive, strategic, inquisitive, courageous, empathetic, enthusiastic, equitable, open-minded, and respectful." The college has created a chart to assess how well its students exhibit these dispositions, and the chart makes clear that a disposition cannot be determined by a specific action or situation but must be judged by a pattern of behavior over one's college career.

Journal Entry: Identifying Your Learning Objectives

For this journal entry, you will need to consider a specific career path, discipline, or major. If you have already determined your major, use that discipline when answering the following questions in your journal. If you have not yet selected a major, pick a discipline that you are considering and use that when answering the questions. If you have multiple majors, you can answer the questions for one of them or all of them; answering the questions for all of them may be quite helpful to you in assessing the full range of learning tasks ahead of you.

- What are the categories of knowledge that are important to learn for someone studying your major?

- What are some specific examples of knowledge you need to learn?

- What are the critical skills to develop for someone pursuing this major?

- What dispositions do you think will lead to success in this area, and why?

---

[3] Ron Ritchhart, *Intellectual Character: What It Is, Why It Matters, How to Get It* (San Francisco, CA: Jossey-Bass, 2002), pp. 18, 31.

Intentional Inquiry: Becoming an Active Learner

One of the most powerful tools for accelerating and directing your learning is **intentional inquiry**. There are two parts to this process. By "intentional," we mean something that is planned, thought through, and decided upon in advance. Earlier we talked about Mike Bell's STIC Method—a habit he has intentionally developed. By "inquiry," we mean inquiring or asking questions. Thus, intentional inquiry is a routine that involves pausing at specific times or in specific circumstances to examine a situation, and then using specific, focused questions to process current information or gather new information.

The journal entry you just completed, in which you answered questions about the knowledge, skills, and dispositions you might need for success in your chosen field, is an example of intentional inquiry. You may have wondered about some of those questions before, but by pausing to reflect and answer those questions in your journal, you have engaged in intentional inquiry.

Raising the right questions and seriously answering them, whether they require personal reflection or seeking out the answers, helps bring clarity to your goals and your tasks. Asking directed questions can help you understand your emotional commitments more fully, enhance your intellectual capacity, and find ways to deal with the practical challenges of implementing your plans.

Intentional inquiry is an ongoing route to acquiring new knowledge and processing existing knowledge. One way to ensure that your inquiry is intentional is to use a structure for asking questions. The most common structure would be to ask questions around specific categories such as time, resources, or habits. Organizing information into categories helps us process knowledge and data more easily.

The Six Steps of Intentional Inquiry

The process outlined in this section is a model you can use to ask directed questions when faced with a situation, challenge, problem, or opportunity. The more you apply this model, the more you may find it valuable in various settings. Driven by your personal Life Wedge, the six steps of intentional inquiry can systematically help empower your personal success efforts and sustain your existing power to accomplish your goals.

The model looks at things from the perspective of three levels: the personal level, the professional level, and the programmatic level. Let's take a closer look at all three.

PERSONAL QUESTIONS. These questions are about finding an emotional connection to the issue at hand.

1. **What is your personal interest?** Do you have a personal stake in the situation or challenge? How does this make you feel? Why?

2. **Is there a pattern to your answers?** Have you answered these kinds of questions in similar ways through the years? What patterns do you notice

in your answers to the questions about this subject? Does this pattern reflect any tendencies or preferences? How can knowledge of these help you make better decisions?

PROFESSIONAL QUESTIONS. These questions are more intellectual, and focus more on gathering specific information to help you deal with the situation or scenario.

3. **What new information is needed?** What key information would help inform your decisions? What new information have you gathered in looking at this situation?

4. **What related information is known or needed?** What other sources of knowledge would provide valuable information? How does what you see relate to what you know? Can you draw any conclusions based on related information?

PROGRAMMATIC QUESTIONS. These questions are practical—they're about putting what you've learned about your emotional response and your professional knowledge into action and helping you develop a strategy and plan.

5. **What is the application?** In what ways will the information you have gathered help you in reaching your life goal or passion? What other application possibilities exist?

6. **How do your abilities fit?** In what ways will your skills allow you to act on this information? What skills or abilities do you need to develop to further act on this information or handle this situation? Where can you learn or develop these?

Throughout college, you're building your knowledge base, constantly increasing your ability to create big pictures for processing learning in other areas. Intentional inquiry is a way to direct some of that learning and processing of information. These six steps are a good routine to apply if you find yourself stuck or confused. While they might not immediately lead to a solution, they can often start you down the right path. And, by helping you take a step back and ask stimulating questions, intentional inquiry also provides a regular energy boost to your journey.

Plato's "Allegory of the Cave"

Imagine, if you will, a deep, dark cave in which prisoners have been chained since birth. They are chained in such a way that they cannot see the fire burning behind them—but they can see images that appear as shadows on the wall before them. (See Figure 7.1 to visualize this better.)

These shadows are cast from items that their captors pass in front of the fire. Over the years, the prisoners have developed a game in which they have named the shadows on the wall, and prisoners take great pride in how quickly and accurately they can identify these shadows.

FIGURE 7.1   Plato's Cave

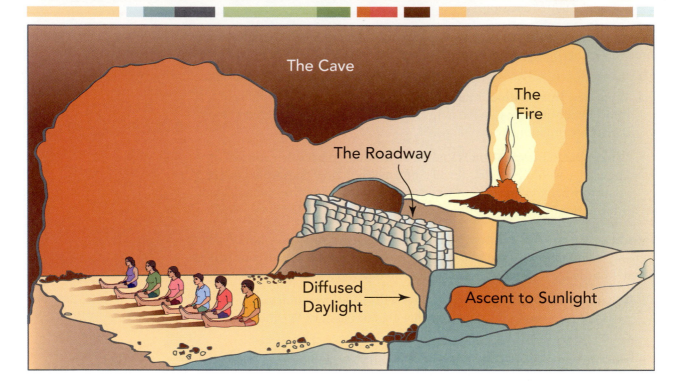

One day, however, a prisoner escapes and emerges into the bright light of the world outside the cave. At first, he is blinded by the natural light, and unaccustomed to seeing anything beyond shadows, he has difficulty identifying what he sees. But soon his eyes acclimate to his new surroundings, and he sees things—rocks, sticks, animals—that he had only ever seen in shadow. Realizing how different the real things are from their shadows, he understands how little he actually knew when he was chained in the cave.

He's faced with a dilemma: stay in the sunlight and live with the fullness of information, or descend again into the cave and attempt to convince his fellow prisoners of the truth they are missing. He knows how powerful it was for him to see things in the real light, but he knows that life in the cave is based on a different system of values, built up over time, and that suggesting to the cave-dwellers that their way of life is wrong will likely bring ridicule. What to do?

Ascending and Descending: Interpreting the Allegory

An allegory is an extended metaphor, presented in story form, that illustrates a principle or moral. The Greek philosopher Plato (427–347 BC) included his "Allegory of the Cave" in *The Republic*, his book that outlines how society should function.

Plato used this story to talk about learning journeys, the challenges that come with learning new things, and how we relate to others once we have acquired new knowledge. The prisoner who escaped to the sunlight was at first overwhelmed by what he saw—he was so used to the darkness of the cave that the bright natural light hurt his eyes, and he needed time to adjust. Things he had learned in the cave over the years, such as how to identify the shadows on the wall, were no help to him in this new environment.

Have you ever had a learning experience in which you felt overwhelmed by the new knowledge or new environment to which you were exposed? When faced with ideas or information that challenge our experience of truth or reality, we may initially resist, preferring to cling to the comfort of what we know. However, as we live with this new information long enough to grow comfortable with it, if it holds up under closer examination in this new light, we can learn to accept it and embrace it. This process may not be quick or easy, but once we come to understand the new knowledge, we look back on our old perceptions differently—we realize those thoughts and opinions were incomplete, uninformed, uneducated, or immature. With our new knowledge, we are a new person; we have ascended, or elevated ourselves, to a new level.

Coming to college is an ascending experience. While in high school, many students feel limited and constrained, like the prisoners in the cave. Yet for all the restrictions that go with the high school experience, there is comfort in the familiarity we find there: We've learned the rules, we know the systems and social conventions, and we understand what to expect in different situations. Over the course of our time in high school, we adapt to those constraints and develop ways to work within them.

Once we arrive at college, though, that familiarity is lost. Expectations change, old social circles are no more, and there are new places to go and new rules to remember for even the simplest things. Our surroundings are different, and adjusting to this environment takes time. Some people, eager to escape the limitations of high school, acclimate quickly, but others, perhaps less open to change, struggle to find their way. Older students also can have a few awkward weeks in nontraditional programs before finding a second home. However, in programs with cohorts (appointed groups that often stay together for two to four years of the college program), they establish rather close support groups and look forward to evenings in class in a familiar building.

Eventually, most people get comfortable with their new life at college. They get excited about learning new ideas, trying new things, and meeting new people. Soon, they *are* new people, with new ways of seeing the world and a new perspective on the world in which they used to live.

So what happens when we go back to that other world, where our "former self" lived? I know many students who, after only a few months at college, have found their first trip back home difficult and awkward. They've become so used to their new life and new environment so quickly that, like the prisoner in the allegory who returned to the cave and struggled to see in the darkness once again, they have trouble readjusting to a place that was once completely familiar to them. The same is often true for older students during the workweek as they attempt to discuss new learning with colleagues with far less education (many of whom are not taking advantage of their company's educational benefits, which often pay for tuition fees).

It's tempting to see people back home or at a certain level in our workplace as "stuck" there. It's also tempting to think that because we've ascended to a new way of seeing things and a new level of education that we've "seen the light." But in reality, all of us are on an educational journey, and we all have things to learn and things we can teach others. Understanding this encourages us to pursue opportunities that may help us ascend and to have humility in situations in which we might feel we have descended.

It's easy to have enthusiasm in a descending situation—you've learned something new that you think will help others, and you're excited to share that information, to teach others what you have been taught so they can have the positive experience you had. In these situations, maintaining humility is much more challenging but no less essential. Not everyone is ready to be taught by someone previously considered a peer, and not every person excited about new knowledge knows how to share that knowledge effectively. I certainly don't want to discourage you from sharing what you've learned—but you should know that in the allegory, when the prisoner returned to the cave and tried to tell his former fellow prisoners how wrong they had been all those years, and that the knowledge they had accumulated was useless, they did not react kindly: They killed him. So no matter how inspired you might be, also remember to be patient and humble because not everyone will be equally ready to accept your lessons.

Of course, many of us go to college precisely so we can descend back to our communities and help lift them up. We often find international students pursuing college degrees in the United States so they can return to their home countries and provide help. I had the privilege of meeting a student from Ensenada, Mexico, where I had visited on a short-term trip to help a service organization. The student had entered the United States to study in Texas, hoping to learn well drilling and understand underground water patterns. Various communities in Ensenada need at least one well, and in one "squatters' city" of many thousands, the Weehawken Indian occupants didn't have a single water well. Those citizens certainly hoped that student could return from college with knowledge and skills that would help improve their lives.

In a similar situation, my colleagues and some of their students had the joy of being in Jembo, Zambia, for the dedication of the village's first well, constructed in conjunction with World Hope International. Those present relayed that the ceremony was both joyous and emotional because that single well would end the daily necessity of four-hour round-trip treks to get water. These treks, always taken by girls or women (many widowed due to AIDS), began before sunrise and were often threatened by attackers, snakes, and wild boars—and sometimes the water source was dry when they arrived, making the trip unproductive. By sharing the knowledge and skills they had gained with those who needed them most, those students and their professors had created what they called an "unforgettable, life-changing experience" for the villagers—and their lives were changed as well.

I have also encountered students from the United States traveling to study in other countries, either for a short period or for an entire degree, to learn skills that have been pioneered or perfected in these countries. For example, I worked with a student from rural Indiana who studied in Japan to understand manufacturing patterns. She anticipated that in an increasingly global economy, her community might soon realize the need for advanced processes and practices that will help it compete globally and ensure its economic survival.

7.1 Ascending Moment

Think of an experience you've had that was an ascending moment for you. In this activity, describe the experience, as well as the main lesson or concept you learned. Then, take a few moments to identify what sparked the learning experience and how you responded to it.

Instance: _____

_____

Main lesson or concept learned: _____

_____

Reason for learning (check all that apply):

_____ Sought out the new knowledge because of curiosity

_____ Sought out the new knowledge because of need, perceived benefit, or potential application

_____ New knowledge was in itself engaging, caught your attention

_____ Medium in which it was packaged was well done, such as a gifted lecturer or teacher, a poignant poem, a provocative film, or a well-written book

_____ Were introduced to questions you had not previously considered

_____ Were introduced to answers you had not previously considered

Your response (check all that apply):

_____ Felt or showed excitement during the learning

_____ Internalized the learning; learning caused you to think further

_____ New knowledge prompted new questions

_____ Made mental notes about the experience

_____ Made literal notes during or after the experience such as notes in class, in a personal journal or notebook, on a blog

_____ Sought more information on the topic

7.2   Descending Moment

For this activity, think of an experience that was a descending moment for you. First, describe the instance in which you attempted to share new knowledge with someone who had a different learning experience and the main lesson, concept, or points you attempted to share. Second, take a few moments to identify why you wanted to share what you had learned and how the listener responded to it.

Instance: _____

_____

Main lesson, concept, or points being shared: _____

_____

Reason for sharing (check all that apply):

_____   Personal excitement about the new knowledge

_____   Expected the listener to find it an interesting topic of discussion

_____   Thought that the new knowledge would benefit the listener in some way

_____   Wanted to help the listener with knowledge as you had been helped

Response of the listener (check all that apply):

_____   Showed excitement about the new information

_____   Seemed to find it of possible value in improving his/her life

_____   Asked questions about how to apply it or how to learn more

_____   Seemed relatively uninterested

_____   Seemed unable to understand the information

_____   Seemed unable to understand the value of the information, or relevance to his/her life situation

_____   Resisted or disagreed with new knowledge or information

_____   Seemed irritated that you were trying to share the information

Finally, what did you learn from the experience of trying to share new knowledge? How might you approach a similar situation differently in the future?

_____

_____

From Knowledge to Power: Learning to Act

In this chapter, we've examined many steps in the learning process: different types of learning, how to apply intentional inquiry to become a more active learner, and the ascending and descending experiences we all have as learners. But as valuable as learning is in its own right, learning alone is not enough for us to achieve success. It is when we put learning into action that knowledge becomes personal power.

Routines are critical for putting learning into action. Often, because learning involves concepts and theories, we process it at a Context or Canvas Level. Routines, however, happen at the Brush-Stroke Level, where we live our lives every day. Think back to Mike Bell and his STIC Method. Mike possessed plenty of knowledge about golf; throughout his lifetime, he had learned about swing mechanics, putting techniques, and other game strategies. But putting that knowledge into action required a simple, concrete, repeatable routine—his STIC Method.

A Reminder to Act: One Student's Life Wedge Story

James Freed stepped away from an established career in public policy to attend college as an adult. Unlike a traditional first-year student, James arrived on campus with considerable life experience. However, like many typical 18-year-old students, he found many distractions once he hit campus.

What helped James find his focus and establish a success plan—one that helped him avoid failing college altogether during his rocky first year on campus—was a simple reminder to act that he placed in his college apartment.

The e-mail from James, excerpted here, talks about that reminder, a simple Brush-Stroke-Level routine he used to keep himself on the path he wanted to travel. The e-mail is addressed to Dr. Brad Garner, our Associate Dean for Student Success, and me. We both gave oversight to the first-year seminar class that James attended.

> **From:** james.freed
>
> **Sent:** Wed 4/18/2007 3:43 PM
>
> **To:** Pattengale, Jerry; Garner, Brad
>
> **Subject:** My Life Wedge
>
> Dr. Garner and Dr. Pattengale,
>
> . . . . I want both of you to know that I take the Life Wedge concept very seriously. It has provided me with clarity when I greatly needed it.

Before I came to Indiana Wesleyan University I was working in a high level of public policy. My work gave me the opportunity to see two worlds. First, I got to see a world in which people had so much. I dined with heads of states, watched history being made on assembly floors, and watched as single votes changed the lives of many. However, the second world I saw was not as glamorous.

In this second world I have seen the struggles of many. I have seen extreme poverty first hand. I have spoken to those who have nothing but the love for their family, and the desire to see their children live a better life than they did. I have walked through the ghettos of this nation, while at the same time walking the halls of the statehouse, and the capital. In these two worlds I have seen problems and solutions, and for the last five years I have strived to find a nexus between the two.

As I look around the world today I see great problems and great challenges. Yet, here I sit at one of the best universities in the world. I feel a bit like Esther in the Old Testament. How scared and confused she must have been. As she sat in the king's palace, she must have asked herself, "who am I and why am I here?" For the last several years I have been asking myself those same questions.

However, [... there's] a call on my life, and that is to continue my work in public policy. Everyday I wake up and look at that simple Life Wedge poster and remind myself where I am going and why I am here. When I get confused and stressed, I simply glance over and remind myself why I am here and where I am going.

I have a role model named Lisa Sullivan. I have never met her, just read about her. She grew up in a working class home in Washington, D.C., and she earned a PhD from Yale. She turned down many job offers to go to New York City and work with "The Forgotten Children of Color." When she would hear people ask, "Where is the next JFK, or Martin Luther King, Jr., or Roosevelt?" she would declare, "We are the ones we have been waiting for!"

Those words haunt me daily. As I look at the problems in the world, and at the same time I see the solutions, I feel [... my] responsibility [is] to be the nexus between the two. [Like the words in the book of Esther] "For such a time as this" ... The task is simply mine to do. I am the nexus I have been searching for.

Now a new generation is rising, and asking the same questions as every generation that has come before it. Who are we? Why are we here? And where are we going? It is my goal, and my Life Wedge still points me there, that I must lead my generation in assuming the responsibilities God has endowed to us. The challenges today are the calling of our time.

—*James Freed (used with permission)*

After receiving this e-mail, we learned that James and his housemates had posted a Life Wedge poster in the living room of their apartment and continually charted activities for one another—often for a specific project or for a particular roommate or friend. At times, they have a lot of fun with wild goals for people and unrealistic wedge activities. But as you can gather from this unsolicited e-mail, they also often had rather serious discussions about the challenges they faced. It seems clear that the daily, visible reminder of his Life Wedge has had a positive impact on James and helped him establish positive routines that have served him well in his academic efforts. I'm happy to report that James is doing rather well today, having gone from near academic failure to excellence. Also, within a year after graduation he became the Village Manager for Lakeview, Michigan, one the youngest chief administrative officers in the nation.

Journal Entry: E-Mail Exercise

In your journal answer the following questions:

- If you were to send an e-mail like the one James sent about your college experience thus far, what member(s) of the faculty, administration, or staff would you send it to? Why?

- What would you share in that e-mail that has helped you the most in your college journey?

- What would you share that has helped you the most in looking beyond college? What class, assignment, or program has a clear application to your future plans?

- When you've answered these questions, write the e-mail. Use the e-mail program you use to compose the note.

Because this is an exercise, I didn't put "send the e-mail" as your final task. However, I strongly encourage you to consider actually addressing the e-mail to the person you identified, and then actually hitting "send" when you've finished. I know what a positive impact that unexpected e-mail from James had on Dr. Garner and me, and I also know that the e-mail provided valuable feedback that we have been able to use to improve the class. Since the e-mail will already be written, you'll be just the push of a button away from sharing your thoughts with someone who has made a difference to you and possibly having an impact on a course or program that will affect students at your school in the future.

Assessment: Evaluating Action, Directing Learning

A key element of achieving our goals is understanding if our actions are indeed making a difference in moving us toward them. Are our practices and rituals actually effective or the most effective actions we could be taking? Is what we label important and believe to be important indeed important to our success?

You could argue that a golfer like our friend Mike Bell has an easy tool for evaluating his effectiveness: his score. But even in golf, where tournaments are won and lost by single strokes, the scorecard is not the only measure of effectiveness. You can play well, applying your knowledge and skills as you set out to do, and still end up with a poor score, perhaps because you caught a few bad bounces or played on an especially tough course. At the same time, you can catch a few lucky bounces and shoot a good score, even if you don't perform particularly well.

In that case, your good score isn't an indicator of strong skills or execution; it's an irregularity, and it holds no promise of success in the future. If you understand that, you won't be satisfied with the good score alone—you'll work to improve your skills and execution to become a consistently good golfer, not someone who occasionally, and randomly, plays a good round of golf.

Thus, an effective evaluation of a golf game involves not only a review of the score but an **assessment** of the actions you took that led to that score. While most golfers set a goal of a specific score, the best golfers also set specific goals for the actions they consistently want to perform that they believe will lead to their desired score. They identify the routines they want to follow that will let them put the lessons they've learned into practice, and after they play, they determine how effectively they followed those routines and if those routines produced the desired outcome. They often practice immediately after a match.

The same principle applies to you in your learning process. Many students simply evaluate themselves on the basis of their score or grade on a paper or test. But does that truly reflect learning? Does it accurately assess your ability to act on what you've learned? Does it demonstrate effective study skills that serve as the foundation for learning in the future? I would argue that any score or grade is an incomplete assessment. To measure effectiveness, you must also examine the actions you performed that led to that score.

How can you examine the actions? To begin, you must set goals for those actions, just like you would set a goal for a grade. Consider all of the things that contribute to that grade: attending class; being attentive and contributing in class; taking notes; reading assigned materials; reviewing your notes; preparing study tools and guides; attending study sessions, labs, and work groups . . . the list goes on. If you have set goals for each of these elements of the learning process, you can evaluate how effectively you achieved those goals, not rate your performance solely on a grade. Based on your evaluation, you can then work to improve those elements that will help you become a consistently strong student, not someone who occasionally and randomly does well on an exam.

Certainly, if you set high standards for yourself in all those areas, achieve those standards, and still receive a poor grade, you may need to evaluate your approach to learning more closely. Perhaps your goals were not the right goals, in that achieving those goals does not correlate with academic success. Perhaps you need to learn more about how you learn and seek additional help in developing proper study skills.

But in my experience, those students who set goals for the different aspects of the learning process, understand how those aspects contribute to their grade, and work to achieve those learning goals and not just a grade goal—in other words, those students who take ownership of their education—rarely receive poor grades.

Journal Entry: Learning Assessment

When you set academic goals, do you focus on outcomes such as grades or inputs such as class attendance, effective note taking, time spent studying, and the like? In your journal, identify five key elements that contribute to learning, and identify at least one goal for each of these elements that you think will help you learn and become a stronger student. When considering these elements and related goals, identify things that, if done consistently well, you believe will lead to better grades.

Once you have identified those goals, write down a routine that you can perform that will help you achieve each goal. A sample routine could be recopying your notes after each class to help you review the material and reinforce what you learned.

Chapter 7 Review

SUMMARY OF MAJOR CONCEPTS

- Routines are the habits we employ to turn ideas and learning into action.

- We can develop routines by default (unintentionally) or by design (intentionally). Routines we develop by design, for a specific purpose, are more effective in helping us achieve our goals.

- A true educational experience is both social and academic, including learning inside and outside the classroom.

- Learning can be divided into three categories: knowledge, skills, and dispositions.

- Knowledge is a key building block for careers, but skills and dispositions are needed to use it effectively and consistently.

- Intentional inquiry is a tool that helps us systematically approach new information.

- When we learn something new, we have an "ascending" experience, and our perspective on where we came from is never the same.

- Having knowledge isn't a license to help others, as not everyone is ready to be taught by someone previously considered a peer, and not everyone who is excited about new knowledge knows how to share it effectively.

- While learning is valuable, acting on what you have learned is necessary to attain success.

- Assessment of your action is an effective way to evaluate what you have learned and improve your performance.

KEY TERMS

STIC Method   a routine that includes four distinct steps: stop, think, imagine, and commit.

default   something (such as a routine) that has evolved unintentionally over time.

design   to develop something (such as a routine) intentionally, through planning and decision making.

knowledge   the category of learning that involves facts, formulas, dates, names, and so forth; sometimes called the "what" of learning.

skills   the category of learning that involves mastery of techniques or application of knowledge; sometimes called the "how" of learning.

disposition   a mindset, outlook, or attitude; a tendency to exhibit a pattern of behavior directed toward a goal; sometimes called the "why" of learning.

Academic Skills   skills such as logic, critical reasoning, and reading that are essential to all academic disciplines.

Communication Skills   interpersonal and group skills that include speech, listening, interacting with others in conversation, social dialogue, small-group interaction, large-group interaction, mass communication, writing, and so on.

Trade Skills   also known as professional skills or skilled trades, these include a variety of learned techniques such as managing stock portfolios or welding.

intentional inquiry   a process of planned questioning; a routine that involves pausing at specific times or in specific circumstances to examine a situation, and then using specific, focused questions to process current information or gather new information.

assessment   an evaluation that reviews outcomes as well as inputs and helps determine a path for future action.

APPLICATION EXERCISE

Learning into Action

Throughout the chapter, we've talked about ways we learn, as well as learning to act on that learning. In this exercise, identify at least four things that you have learned in the last year that you have applied through specific action. Next, determine whether what you learned can be categorized as knowledge, a skill, or a disposition. Finally, in the third column, describe the action you performed that was made possible by what you learned.

What You Learned	Category of Learning: Knowledge, Skill, or Disposition	Action You Performed, Made Possible by This Learning

After you complete this exercise, answer the following questions:

- Which category of learning was more likely to lead to action on your part?

- Why do you think that is?

- What have you learned about your learning habits and experiences from this assessment?

REMINDER

In this chapter we read of James Freed and his roommates' use of the Life Wedge poster. For James, the poster was a last-resort approach to remaining in school, and it worked. And, as he notes, it's now become his first resort, something he reviews each morning. Have you considered a way of making the Life Wedge a part of *your* daily routine? We all have habits and schedules, and many deadlines. Sometimes these habits distract us from what's most important. James developed a habit that supported his goals and efforts. Are you cultivating habits that help you stay on track with your goals?

8 Writing Your Own Story: The Power of Purpose

Common Folks Can Bring Uncommon Blessings

My neighbor Harold punched James Dean.

The 6′4″ teenager just couldn't take the little gadfly any more.

"He just kept pestering me, and I kept warning him," recounted Harold. "I warned him, 'Now, Jimmy, if you don't quit, I'm going to have to hit you.' He didn't stop, and so I punched him in the stomach."

The fun-loving Harold, now retired, continues, "After I hit him, Jimmy bent over, then said, 'Harold, that was a good one.'" Harold laughs when asked to retell the story about "Little Jimmy," whom he calls a "piece of work."

Jimmy, according to the man who lived his whole history within 10 miles of Dean's home, "was just one of the boys" but "was always up to something— always full of energy."

During the fall of 1948, Harold Mart and the rest of Fairmount High had no idea that the wiry, bent-over, flat-topped, horn-rimmed Jimmy would one day become James Dean, legendary pompadoured alumnus. And Jimmy, restless and full of life, didn't know that the fist that hit him in the gut that day would farm the fields of Fairmount, Indiana, for 60 years after his own body would be placed six feet under.

James Dean left his Fairmount farm and traveled the country. Harold Mart stayed on his Fairmount farm and has rarely left the county.

James Dean lived on the edge and wanted to plow new ground. Harold Mart plowed the same ground into his seventies.

James Dean would become identified with a red Porsche Spider. Harold Mart can be found in a faded blue, four-door Pontiac Bonneville with over 178,000 miles on it.

James Dean wore jeans and a T-shirt, with his hallmark cigarette dangling from his lip. You might catch Harold Mart in a T-shirt, but not to show off his physique—rather, to cool down after mowing. For Harold, being cool takes priority over looking cool.

James Dean would provide the motivation for thousands of people to drive their classic Mercury coupes to Fairmount every year. Harold Mart's home draws a few cars a year, too—usually for strawberries or hay, or to borrow a tool.

James Dean spawned posters and neon signs. Harold Mart isn't exactly poster material—and neither Wal-Mart nor Kmart is named for my neighbor.

James Dean became a heartthrob to millions of young women. Harold Mart gave his heart to one woman—Marcella, his wife of 55 years.

James Dean pursued Hollywood and found it. Harold Mart pursued heaven and will never lose it.

James Dean became the famous "Rebel without a Cause." Harold Mart became Harold.

James and Harold took divergent paths from the halls of Fairmount High, but both of their lives are worthy of our attention. The adventure and risk of a Hollywood hunk perks our ears and stirs our curiosity. The stable surefooted-ness of a lifetime farmer sounds calm and secure in a hectic world.

Unlike my little hometown of Buck Creek, Fairmount still has its old brick high school—not because it has a daily function in the community, or because it's a priceless piece of architecture, or even because it's where Harold Mart earned his diploma. No, the school still stands because James Dean once roamed those halls. When he died in 1955, Fairmount was born in the world's eyes.

I recently visited Buck Creek, less than an hour's drive west from Dean's gravestone. Unlike Fairmount, our town boasts no legendary names or stories of Hollywood adventure, and no celebrity cause saved our high school. However, there are Harolds—plenty of them—who have maintained their farms and livelihoods within a few miles of their childhood homes. And each of them likely knows the story of James Dean—the life of adventure, fun, and risk, of throwing caution to the wind.

While most counties have their share of Harolds, the entire country shares one James Dean, and, in the end, that's for the best. Sure, it's good to have a few wandering, carefree adventurers to stoke our restlessness and inspire us to dream. But if the ratio was flipped, and stable, loyal, caring, committed citizens were the uncommon ones, our communities would be chaotic. We'd have to run want ads to find responsible people to hold public office and teach our children, and we'd certainly have fewer, if any, family farms.

James Dean lets us have wild dreams. Harold Mart helps us see the reality of responsibility. James appeals to youthful desires; Harold, to the desire to help our youth.

A while back, I was the guest speaker at Fairmount's "Legends Diner" on Main Street, to read some of my stories and provide a motivational challenge to an older group, nearly all contemporaries of James Dean. The room, draped in James Dean wallpaper and historic Dean pictures, was full, but sitting head and shoulders above the crowd was 71-year-old Harold Mart.

Afterward, Harold asked my wife and me to go for a ride. Not far north of Fairmount, he pulled into a cemetery and drove us to Dean's graveside. "Jimmy was a good boy," said Harold. "I thought you'd like to see his stone." Then he pointed east a hundred feet or so, just above James' simple pinkish stone, to two simple grave markers that read "Mart." Harold had purchased them 30 years earlier, to ensure a local and debt-free resting place. He knew where he was born, and he knew where he would be buried—he just didn't know when.

As we drove away, Harold pointed out the farm where Little Jimmy worked, and then throughout the countryside he pointed to many places where homes of friends once stood and where memories still lived. Riding down those country roads, it hit me that even though few people outside of Fairmount knew or would ever know the name of Harold Mart, his life—purposeful, disciplined, simple, and focused—was more inspiring and meaningful to me than that of any star of the silver screen. Just as his fist had once connected with the gut of the famous James Dean, Harold's life had connected solidly, deep within me. "Harold," I thought to myself, "that was a good one."

The life of a James Dean? Fascinating.

The life of a Harold Mart? Motivating.[1]

How Will Your Story Read?

I suspect Harold Mart never gave much thought to his life story—he grew up expecting he would be a farmer, and that's the life he lived, according to the values instilled in him as a child on the farm.

As a college student in an interconnected world, your situation is probably quite different from Harold's. Whether you've chosen a career path or are still undecided, your degree will open many doors and create many opportunities for you. The storyline of your life could go in many different directions.

Yet whether you've thought about it this way or not, the first few chapters of your life story have already been written. This book is about determining how the rest of those chapters will read.

We began our journey together by examining dreams: how dreams can guide us, how obstacles can get in our way, and how the dream must be stronger than the struggle. Using the idea of the Life Wedge, we've looked at how focus, discipline, and intentional effort can help us move toward achieving those dreams.

We've studied heroes and their noble causes, connected class work to our Life Wedge, examined the forces of willpower and waypower, and analyzed the impact of hope and perseverance on our dreams. We've stepped back to see the big picture, and considered what it means to take ownership of our education. In summary, we've developed essential tools and learned about mindsets and strategies that will help us write the next chapters of our life stories.

Of course, life won't always follow the script we write for it. But determining a script and applying our Life Wedge to it is a formula for working purposefully toward mature dreams. Failing to write a script, failing to construct a Life Wedge, failing to identify a driving purpose—these are formulas for aimless wandering and dreams that remain forever immature.

---

[1] A version of this story originally appeared in the *Marion Chronicle Tribune*, January 18, 2004.

As this book comes to a close, I want to focus on the idea that is at the core of *The Purpose-Guided Student*: purpose.

The Central Role of Purpose

To understand the impact that a sense of purpose can have on your education and development, let's look at the impact purpose can have on an institution: your college. Every college has a **mission statement**, which is a statement of purpose or declaration of intent that explains why the college exists—what its purpose is, what its aims are, and how it intends to achieve those aims. Take a moment now to find your college's mission statement. You should be able to find it on your school Web site; if you don't see "Mission Statement" listed in the site navigation (often under the "About" header), it might be called "Statement of Purpose," "Vision Statement," or something similar. You also might look in your college catalog.

Once you find your college mission statement, write it out in the space below:

The Official Mission Statement of Your College or University
Your Initial Reaction to This Mission Statement (Use Adjectives)

A mission statement is a public declaration; it says to the world, "This is what we stand for as an institution." Because that mission is public, it creates accountability—it tells students, faculty, alumni, accrediting organizations, and others what they can expect from the college, and it invites them to measure the college against the standard it has set for itself.

In the journal entry assignment below, take a few moments to examine your college's mission statement, and then evaluate it based on your experience as a student there.

Journal Entry: Analyzing Your College's Mission

Read over your college's mission statement again, and then answer the following questions in your journal.

- Based on your reading of your college's mission statement, what do you believe are your school's top three priorities?

- Based on your experience as a student at your college, how has the school demonstrated commitment, through specific actions or choices, to these priorities?

- How does your school measure how well it is living up to its mission? What standards or evaluation tools could be used to hold the school accountable to its stated mission?

- How has the history, heritage, character, or personality of your school been shaped by this mission statement? How has the mission statement been shaped by the history, heritage, character, or personality of your school?

- How have the college's efforts to live its mission impacted your experience as a student there?

Purpose in Practice on Campus

Earlier we discussed the research of psychologist Frederick Herzberg, whose examination of workplace motivation led him to argue that "the opposite of 'Satisfaction' is 'No Satisfaction,' and the opposite of 'Dissatisfaction' is 'No Dissatisfaction. . . . to eliminate factors that create job dissatisfaction can bring about peace, but not necessarily motivation."[2] From these findings comes what I have termed the Herzberg Principle, which declares that "removing dissatisfaction does not lead to intrinsic motivation."

Yet despite Herzberg's extensive research, I see many campuses today whose efforts to increase student satisfaction still focus on removing dissatisfaction. As a result, they improve the food, the living arrangements, and the parking but fail to address the motivation of the students, many of whom still crave something more meaningful than anything that can be found on a cafeteria menu.

I have seen something different on my campus. More than a decade ago, we developed a program that focused on helping students determine their life purpose. Research that tracked the progress of students participating in this purpose-guided initiative revealed that the approach has led to around 20 percent increases in retention rates and four-year graduation rates since 1998.[3] In other words, emphasizing the importance of purpose has helped keep students in school and on the path to success.

In developing the program, faculty determined that undeclared students may be at a higher risk of having motivation issues, so we developed a class targeted specifically at them that focused on determining life purpose. Students who took this class were up to *six times* more likely to have earned their degree at the end of four years than those who did not take the class.

Our campus is not alone in experiencing this purpose phenomenon. Extensive research shows that students who have a general understanding of their life purpose (and, as a result, the purpose of their education) are much more likely to find success in college. They are also likely to develop a viable plan for a career path—one that will provide earning power as well as personal fulfillment.[4]

---

[2] Stephen P. Robbins, *Organizational Behavior*, 8th ed. (Upper Saddle River, NJ: Prentice Hall, 1998).

[3] Jerry Pattengale, "Purpose-Guided Education: Student Success or Student Non-Dissatisfaction," plenary address, *Indiana Chapter of the National Association of Developmental Education,* Indianapolis, October 28, 2005. Published in *Growth,* 6 (Spring 2006): 13-25.

[4] The 2005 study conducted jointly by Indiana University and Indiana Wesleyan University reveals that an intentional curricular program helping students determine their life purpose correlates with radically higher graduation rates (Leaders of the research team include Drs. Edward St. John [University of Michigan], Don Hossler and Jeff McKinney [Indiana University], and Jerry Pattengale and Bill Millard [Indiana Wesleyan University]).

This research is why we've invested so much time examining purpose: Satisfaction and success are achieved through action and effort, action and effort are spurred by motivation, motivation is driven by purpose, and a sense of purpose is encouraged and developed by discussing and giving serious thought to dreams, life goals, and purpose itself.

Chip Anderson, whom we mentioned in the first chapter, summarizes this thinking in a simpler equation:

If the Why is big enough, the How will show up.

Defining the Why: A Personal Mission Statement

Much as your college has crafted a mission statement to explain its purpose and the impact it wants to have on its students and its community, many people write personal mission statements for themselves. A personal mission statement is a way of saying, "This is who I want to be in the world."

The process of developing any mission statement, personal or institutional, involves a great deal of reflection and thought. While people can and do change their personal mission statements, the sentiments they express are not meant to change every week—they are meant to reflect serious purpose and honest commitment.

A mission statement says what you stand for, the values you hold dear, and the mark you want to leave on others. An effective mission statement serves as a measuring stick: It enables you to consider your actions, your behavior, and your character and compare these to what you have outlined in your mission statement to determine whether you are living up to the standard you have set for yourself.

Writing a personal mission statement is a big step toward identifying a *Why* that's big enough to encourage the *How* to show up. If your personal mission is inspiring to you, it can give you a sense of direction and support the efforts of your Life Wedge.

Journal Entry: A Personal Mission Statement

Review your college's mission statement again. What do you notice about its structure? What themes and concepts does it address? How do you think its central values and declarations of purpose were developed?

Once you have considered your college's mission statement, write a personal mission statement for yourself in your journal.

Purpose-Guided Learning

Now that you have articulated your life purpose in a personal mission statement, how does that impact your life as a college student?

I have found that writing a personal mission statement, like drawing a Life Wedge for the first time, can be a jarring experience for many people. Stopping to give serious thought to such major life issues, spelling out your intentions so plainly, and committing those intentions to paper, rather than simply saying them out loud, all tend to cause people to reexamine their behaviors, choices, and activities. Many college students immediately reevaluate something they had previously taken for granted: being a college student.

They start to realize the impact that their time at college can have on achieving their life goals and living their personal mission. Many get uncomfortable thinking about how they have spent their time at college thus far: going to class, yes, but going through the motions more than learning with a purpose. Maybe you're feeling that way a little bit, too.

No matter how you're feeling at this point, you're still in college, and that means you still have the opportunity to learn with a purpose while you're smack in the middle of an incredibly rich learning environment and establish a foundation for lifelong purpose-guided learning.

When you pursue **purpose-guided learning**, what you learn in class stops being disconnected bits of information and becomes new knowledge that you can process and place in context in the light of your mission and goals.

Having a larger purpose to guide your learning also changes how you look at the decisions you make: which classes to take, which extracurricular activities to participate in, how you study, and more.

By Default or By Design

Too often in my life, I've seen someone respond to a situation with "stuff happens" and a shrug. And while I've found it to be true—stuff definitely does happen—I've also come to believe that when that particular phrase (or one like it) becomes a personal motto, and a shrug becomes a regular reaction of resignation to the world around you, it's a good sign you're living your life by default, and not by design.

In the last chapter, we talked about the routines in our lives and whether they are established by default or by design. Routines are not simply isolated quirks that populate our days, however—they are representative snapshots of our lives. The things that make up the big picture of our lives, such as our character, our career, and the noble causes we do or do not pursue, are also determined by default or by design.

Having a Life Wedge, writing a personal mission statement, and committing yourself to purpose-guided learning are all ways of taking responsibility for your life and making sure that your life is lived by design instead of by default. While it's incredibly easy to let a day get away from you, and then a week, and then a month, you do have the power and the ability to take a greater measure of control. Fixing a purpose for your life and your learning is critical to that effort. By discovering your *Why*, you can move more effectively to determine the *How*.

We also talked in the last chapter about the power of ascending moments, those times when we leave our cave and see, hear, or experience something that changes our outlook forever, expanding our minds and challenging our notion of what we know. Often, those ascending moments are unpredictable. One of the most significant ascending moments in my life occurred when my professor drew that "V" on the board and explained the concept of the Life Wedge, back when I was in college. But when I walked into class that day, I had no idea I was about to have an ascending experience. Fortunately, I was aware enough to realize what was happening when it happened and wise enough to act on it.

Ascending moments are not accidental by definition, though. We can choose to take a class, read a book, watch a movie, visit a city, meet a person, or pursue an activity that we know will challenge us. Those challenges represent opportunities to ascend, and the more we take advantage of those opportunities, and put ourselves in position to have ascending moments, the more we can intentionally learn, grow, and stretch ourselves.

Knowing your life purpose can help you identify the kind of ascending experiences you want to have and seek them out. You will still stumble into many ascending moments, I assure you, and these experiences will be no less powerful for their randomness or serendipity. But if you intend to ascend, you'll experience more ascending moments more consistently, which will reinforce and support your efforts to sharpen your Life Wedge and move toward your goals.

Being in the Story

When my four sons were young, I told them bedtime stories every night, each one an epic battle between the forces of good and evil. Every night, a new villain, each more dastardly than the last, would plot to take over or destroy a helpless village, harmless town, or other seemingly defenseless community. And every night, four heroes would rise to the defense of those kind and gentle citizens: Jason, Joshua, Nicholas, and Michael.

My sons were always delighted with the outcome because they were always in the story: Their names are Jason, Joshua, Nicholas, and Michael, too. I never had to worry about them drifting off because each wanted to find out which heroic part he was going to play in helping save the innocent people.

As adults, we still become more engaged in a story when we can see ourselves in it. The bombings in Iraq, the tsunami in Indonesia, or Hurricane Katrina may seem far away, but when we imagine what it would be like to be impacted by these tragedies, we identify with the grief and loss of loved ones. As we pay close attention to the news, search online for more information, and discuss what's happening with friends and relatives, we not only become more informed, we become invested: We think about how we would react, what we can learn, and, even though we may be many miles away, what we can do now to provide support and assistance. We become part of the story ourselves.

Whether we enter uplifting stories or tragic ones, the key to tapping into the power of stories is to engage with them rather than simply be entertained by them. Being in the story helps us become active learners, and every story presents us with an opportunity to apply lessons from its concepts and consequences to our own lives. As alert readers and viewers and observant participants in the world around us, we can take ideas that may seem remote or abstract and connect them to our own experience in a way that enables us to reap the benefits.

As a college student, you will encounter many stories that can serve as either entertainment or an opportunity for engagement. The books you are assigned to read as part of your college curriculum are intended to engage you. They're not assigned randomly or picked by default but rather are identified and chosen very much by design.

Despite the thoughtfulness and intent that goes into determining course content, I often encounter students who respond with a groan when a book identified as a "classic" turns up on a syllabus. I challenge those students to consider why that book is there. Contrary to popular belief, professors do not take special joy in torturing their students. We know that important books are often challenging to read, but we don't include these challenging books in our courses just to achieve a certain degree of difficulty—we put them there with the purpose of challenging your perspective and exposing you to a way of thinking that we believe can be useful and instructive. In other words, we place those books on the syllabus because we believe they will present you with a Crossroads experience.

A student looking only for entertainment might find these classic books "boring" or "hard" and wish for an easier or more exciting text. But a purpose-guided student will look at these books, understand that they have been part of a larger conversation for decades—if not centuries—for a reason, and appreciate that only by reading these books and engaging with them can they understand their role in modern thought and modern culture, as well as why these books have become classics. In fact, students who understand that purpose-guided learning builds on experiences beyond our own will look to find ways to connect those books with their purpose and goals in life and make their encounter with these books a Crossroads experience—by design.

But what about textbooks? The classics, which often define classes in the humanities, have become classics because they resonate with some aspect of the human story. If your college has a "Great Works" curriculum, it is driven by the truths of these timeless texts, and the goal of introducing students in these programs to brilliant authors and some of life's most universal guiding principles.

Textbooks, however, are rarely considered "great works" or "classics." As a writer of textbooks and a devoted fan of the classics myself, I'm well aware that neither this book nor the other textbooks I've written are likely to become classics. That's the nature of textbooks. Yet if our learning is purpose-guided, we will still find a way to stay engaged with textbooks—to find a way to tie in the lessons contained there with our goals and purpose. And when you encounter a book—be it a textbook, a classic, or something somewhere in between—that doesn't immediately draw you in or capture your attention, you might consider applying the **Proximity Principle**.

The Proximity Principle

The Proximity Principle is a simple adage I've developed over the years to remind myself of the need to maintain the right distance from what I'm reading or learning:

> It's difficult to read when you're too close to the page or to continue reading when you're too far from the story.

"Too close to the page" can certainly be taken literally—just bring this particular page up to your eyes until the words blur and you'll see what I mean—but the real proximity we're concerned with is not one of eyeballs as much as emotion and intellect. For example, let's say you've been assigned to read Nathaniel Hawthorne's *The Scarlet Letter*. Hawthorne wrote in a different era from our own, so his vocabulary and cultural references will be different from ones we're used to. If in reading this book you stop at every unknown word to look it up in the dictionary, or put the book down every time you come across a historical nuance that's new to you so you can Google it, not only will it take you forever to finish the book, but you won't be reading the book so much as you'll be scanning words to identify the ones you don't recognize. Bogged down in the details, you'll be too close to the page to understand the big picture of the book, and you'll likely miss the themes and message that make *The Scarlet Letter* a classic.

At the other end of the spectrum—being too far away from the story—we can find ourselves reading the story but never investing ourselves in it. Some students complete their assigned reading quickly, not only because they never stop to look up unfamiliar words but also because they never stop to think about what they're reading and how it relates to them and their learning. Just as being too close to the page can keep you from understanding the impact of what you're reading and applying it to your own experience, so can being a superficial reader. If we feel no connection to a story or assignment, it's difficult to stay engaged and "continue reading."

If something you're reading doesn't immediately grab your attention, pause to ask yourself questions that might help you get closer to the story, such as

- How does what I'm reading connect to my experience?

- If I don't find a personal connection, who among my friends or family might connect to this? Why?

- How might it help me develop empathy for experiences different from mine or people different from me?

- Why was this book assigned to me? What message or lesson does the professor want us to get from reading this book?

- How could this book help me sharpen my Life Wedge?

- What connection could this book have to my life purpose?

When homework or assigned work does not readily appeal to us, it's often because we see no connection to the human story, or, more importantly, to *our story*. Even when an experience or concept does engage our mind, if we don't take time to reflect on it, we'll often forget it or have difficulty articulating its lessons down the road. The Proximity Principle is a reminder to find the right distance from new ideas and new information so we can engage with, learn from, and remember it.

Journal Entry: Applying the Proximity Principle

Think about the books that you have been assigned during this term, and identify one that you didn't connect with, that didn't spark your interest, or that you struggled to read. In your journal, answer the following questions about that book:

- With this book, were you too close to the page or too far from the story?

- How do you think that affected your reading of it?

- How could you have either taken a step back from the page or gotten closer to the story?

- Why do you think the book was assigned to you? How does it fit in with the objectives of the course?

- What lessons could be gained from rereading or reconsidering the book at the proper proximity?

A Commitment to Lifelong Learning

One of my favorite paragraphs in all of literature is the one that opens *Travels with Charley*, John Steinbeck's biographical reflections while traveling with his dog:

When I was very young and the urge to be someplace else was on me, I was assured by mature people that maturity would cure this itch. When years described me as mature, the remedy prescribed was middle age. In middle age I was assured that greater age would calm my fever and now that I am fifty-eight perhaps senility will do the job. Nothing has worked. . . . Four hoarse blasts of a ship's whistle still raise the hair on my neck and set my feet to tapping. The sound of a jet, an engine warming up, even the clopping of shod hooves on pavement brings on the ancient shudder, the dry mouth and vacant eye, the hot palms and the churn of stomach high up under the rib cage.

Every time I read that paragraph, I feel that same itch myself. It stirs the sense of adventure deep in my bones and sparks that "urge to be someplace else" in me. It reminds me of my rail travels through Europe when I was 19 and the two years I lived in a cabin in the woods, right out of Henry David Thoreau's *Walden*.

What made those travels and adventures so special and so memorable were the challenges I faced and the discoveries I made along the way, about the world and about myself. I had a lot of fun, yes, but those were also profound learning and growing experiences. They taught me how much I could learn beyond a college campus, and they redefined my idea of what it means to be a lifelong learner.

Perhaps you, too, have experienced travels and adventures that proved to be profound learning experiences. Or maybe travel is not your thing, and you find that you gain more from being alone in nature and having time to think, or exploring different ideas in a library or a bookstore full of books, or finding a physical challenge that pushes you out of your comfort zone.

No matter what you prefer, what's important is to pursue those experiences and to be purposeful in charting a path of **lifelong learning**. Sadly, most people miss out on the grand adventure of pursuing their life purpose. My journals are full of conversations with people whose biggest regret in life is that they stayed with a career path that they fell into rather than one they sought. They never followed their urge to be someplace else. They never took risks.

While speaking in Ireland recently, I serendipitously befriended a physician who was also traveling to some of the famous literary sites near Dublin. Now nearing retirement, he has a wildly successful practice back in the United States, yet when he heard about the Life Wedge, he got very excited about it. In fact, he shared a remarkable admission with me: He had not pursued his life passion but was hoping to start after retirement. When I asked him when he knew he was off track, he said it happened during graduate school, when he changed his major to medicine to avoid being drafted to fight in Vietnam. Although he loves law, and always has, he became too comfortable in a worthy—but disconnected—life path and felt like he couldn't leave it.

Admittedly, it's easy to lose track of long-range goals as family and career obligations make life both more complicated and more regimented. If you let it, travel can become merely an escape for pleasure and relaxation rather than an adventure for development and discovery.

But that path is not for you anymore. You are now on a purpose-guided path, the path of a lifelong learner. Your challenge is to find ways to continue learning, to continue growing, to continue moving forward along the path you have chosen, to continue living with purpose.

As a college student, you are in an ideal environment to practice these habits. The more you make this purpose-guided approach part of your disposition now, the better you will be prepared for the major transition that lies ahead: the transition from college to the rest of your life.

From College to the "Real World"

By the time you graduate from college, you will actually have experienced many transitions. Coming to college in itself is a major transition, and at the end and beginning of every term, you are faced with another transition. Yet the transition that is most intimidating to most people is the transition from college to career, or, as many people say, from college to the "real world."

Part of the reason people joke that life on a college campus is different from the "real world" is that as a college student, a great deal of the institution's attention is focused on you and your peers; indeed, the structure of a typical college campus is designed to support the success of its students. In a career setting, this is not the case.

Elwood Holton, a professor of human resource development, has examined the transition from campus to career settings and notes that the very structure of college can work against people in the transition to post-graduation life. He has identified five major areas in which the difference between life during college and life after college is significant. These areas are outlined next.

1. <u>Direction during College</u>: Students "receive a lot of direction about what to do and how to do it. The curriculum tells them what courses to take, and professors tell them what is expected of them. If the professors do not give a clear syllabus or tell them what to study for an exam, students are probably entitled to get upset."
   <u>Lack of Direction after College</u>: Graduates "rarely get that type of direction at work and are likely to complain."

2. <u>Feedback during College</u>: Students become accustomed to hearing "how they are doing."
   <u>Lack of Feedback after College</u>: Graduates "frequently ask their managers for feedback—leaving the impression that they are insecure."

3. <u>Personal Development during College</u>: Students become accustomed "to growing and developing through education. . . ."
   <u>Lack of Personal Development after College</u>: Graduates "get very upset when their boss does not send them to much training during the first year."

4. <u>Challenging Assignments during College</u>: Students become accustomed to being stretched intellectually.
   <u>Lack of Challenges after College</u>: Graduates fail to realize "that work seldom mimics college."

5. <u>Questioning and Challenging Structures during College</u>: Students spend considerable energy during college challenging established practices at their institution. They are given "class participation" points for challenging professors "(their 'superiors')."
   <u>Questionable Judgment after College</u>: Graduates "are faulted for not using good judgment because they are too quick to challenge established practices in the organization." They are charged for not respecting superiors.

One of the great benefits of taking a Big Picture Approach to life is the ability to handle transitions like this more easily. When you take a Context-Level view of your life, not only do you see that transitions are a necessary part of the Big Picture, but you are less likely to be thrown off course by the details of the transition because you understand that they are not the whole story—they are pieces of something larger, Brush Strokes of a greater painting.

Journal Entry: Looking Forward

As a student in this class, you're required to reflect on notions of purpose, causes, and life goals. However, once you have finished this course, and certainly once you leave the college setting, the curriculum for personal development is self-imposed.

In your journal, reflect on the following questions about the transition from college to the next chapter of your life:

- Which concepts and tools that you have learned in this book do you think will help you in your transition to life after college? Why?

- Describe the biggest challenges you think you will face as you transition from college to your career.

- How do you plan to face those challenges? How can you apply what you have learned in this course to those challenges?

- How can a mindset of lifelong learning and engagement help you achieve success after you leave college? How do you plan to cultivate that mindset of lifelong learning and engagement?

- How can a sense of purpose, like what you've articulated in your personal mission statement, help you with the challenges that come in the transition from college to career?

Journaling: The Value of Reflecting on Your Story

Throughout the course of this book, you've had many journal assignments to complete. In each of these, I've asked you to write down your personal reflections on a topic we've discussed or to relate a personal experience to the subject at hand. Undoubtedly, you enjoyed writing some of these journal entries more than others; my guess is that some felt like busy work, and for these your entries were rather brief, but that for others, you appreciated the opportunity to explore the material we were discussing in greater depth and to find ways to connect it to your own life.

What you may not have considered as you were writing these journal entries is what you were building along the way. Here at the end of the term, if you look back through your journal, you will see that you now have a record of your perspective on the topics of purpose, motivation, and personal development that we discussed in this class. You can look back and see how your thoughts and opinions evolved and grew. You have created a document of who you were and what you were thinking at this point in your life, a set of notes on the chapter of your personal story that took place over the course of this course.

Now that we have come to the end of this class and this book, you won't be getting any more journal entry assignments from me. But will you continue to keep a journal? You probably won't be surprised to find that I think the best way to answer that question is with a journal assignment.

Journal Entry: Reflecting on Your Journal

Take some time to read back through the entries in your journal, going all the way back to the first entries from Chapter 1 at the beginning of the course. Then, answer the following questions in your journal.

- Upon reading your journal entries a second time, which one was most meaningful or significant to you? Why?

- What themes or recurring ideas did you notice when rereading your journal entries? Did you expect these, or were you surprised? Why?

- How did your experience with journaling change over the course of this class? How did you feel about journaling in the beginning of the term? How do you feel about it now?

- What do you see as the benefits of the journaling process? Which of these benefits was most valuable to you over the course of this class?

- Do you think you will continue to keep and use a journal after this class is complete? Why?

- If yes, what do you hope to gain from journaling?

- If no, is there another way you will be able to experience the benefits offered by journaling?

- How can journaling contribute to your lifelong learning?

- If you were to title your journal, like a book, what would you call it? Why?

Closing Thoughts, Opening Questions

Probably more than any other class you will take as a college student, this course has been about you—your goals, your dreams, your Life Wedge, your purpose, your routines, your challenges, your Crossroads experiences, your ascending moments. And while I hope this book has given you some helpful ideas, related some useful stories, offered some valuable suggestions, and provided some insightful answers, more than anything, I hope it has given you plenty of challenging questions.

The questions we addressed throughout the chapters of this book apply not only to this chapter of your life but to all the ones to come. The questions are personal because the answers are personal: While you can draw ideas and inspiration from many places, ultimately you have to find what works for you, not for anybody else. Your purpose must be personal. Your Life Wedge must be personal. Your dreams must be personal.

Of course, no purpose, Life Wedge, or dream will mean much if you do not work at it and regularly check in with yourself to ensure you are making progress toward your desired outcome. One simple step you can take is to mark your calendar at a regular interval, such as the first day of every month, and on that day, pull out your Life Wedge and check in with yourself. On those days, you also may want to consider some of the following questions, which we have asked ourselves through the course of this book:

- How sharp and focused is my Life Wedge?

- What worthy cause am I pursuing?

- What other worthy causes have I seriously considered?

- What cause motivates me to give my best energies to it?

- How can I best develop the appropriate skills for the life goal I've listed?

- Who else is headed in the same direction as I am? What can I learn from them?

- What historic figures inspire me toward my goal, and how?

- How have others stayed focused on their goals?

- How do I know that my Life Wedge is realistic?

- What do I need to add inside my Life Wedge to reach my goal?

- What do I need to remove from inside my Life Wedge to stay focused?

- How often should I revise my Life Wedge?

- How can my current assignments assist me in reaching my life pursuit?

- How am I going to be intentional about my future?

- How will I ensure I am actively pursuing my dreams?

- How do I want my life story to read?

As we come to the final pages, I have three simple wishes for you: I wish you a lifetime of purpose-guided learning. I wish you a sharp, narrow wedge. And I wish for you that while this book is at an end, the class is not.

Chapter 8 Review

SUMMARY OF MAJOR CONCEPTS

- A mission statement, for an individual or an institution, is a declaration of purpose that can be used to guide actions and behaviors.

- Having a Life Wedge, writing a personal mission statement, and committing yourself to purpose-guided learning are all ways of taking responsibility for your life and making sure that your life is lived by design instead of by default.

- The key to tapping into the power of stories is to engage with them rather than simply be entertained by them.

- It is difficult to read when you're too close to the page or to continue reading when you're too far from the story.

- Taking a Big Picture Approach to life helps you handle transitions more easily.

KEY TERMS

mission statement   a statement of purpose or declaration of intent that explains someone's or something's reason for being and avowed aims.

purpose-guided learning   learning that is directed and focused by a specific purpose or objective such as a goal or mission statement.

Proximity Principle   the idea that states, *It's difficult to read when you're too close to the page or to continue reading when you're too far from the story.* A reminder of the need to maintain the right distance, or proximity, from what one is reading or learning.

lifelong learning   an approach that emphasizes continual development and discovery of new ideas and information beyond college and throughout one's lifetime.

APPLICATION EXERCISE:

Write an Op-Ed Piece

In this chapter, we have given serious thought to life purpose. For your final assignment, you're going to write an opinion-editorial article about a topic that relates to your life purpose. You could write about a cause that matters to you, an issue in the news that somehow connects to your purpose or Life Wedge, or something else about which you are passionate.

Op-Ed pieces are honest attempts at discussing substantial questions facing the community or nation as a whole. For samples of this kind of article, pick up your local paper or find the Web site of a newspaper you like, and go to the Opinion or Editorial section.

The following questions and guidelines will help you write your Op-Ed piece. Your target word length is 600 words.

1. **What current issues are related to your life goal or a noble cause of serious interest**? For example, if you have a passion to help people with physical challenges, you might be thinking of going into medicine, nursing, dentistry, chiropractics, physical therapy, or a related field. Is there a current issue that is of interest to your community or in the national dialogue surrounding your area of passion? The list of possible topics related to your likely career field or noble cause is wide ranging.

2. **Begin your article with a Big Picture story** that is either personal or related to the situation.

3. **Determine your thesis**. At the end of the 600 words, what one key thought do you want the reader to walk away with?

4. **Outline the article, beginning with the Big Picture**. You might choose to state your thesis in the first sentence or two to segue into your discussion. If you were writing a research paper, the thesis would likely be up front. Op-Ed pieces allow for more flexibility in structure; what's important is that you engage the reader. Sometimes Op-Eds are most effective when they draw readers into a subject that they may have overlooked or never considered before.

5. **Determine what information is relevant to the key point, including setting the stage through a Big Picture**. While giving an example, some details simply may not be necessary. Economy of words is the issue.

6. **Get in and out of the main point**. Just as quickly as you introduce your key points, choose your words wisely and pack your sentences, then get to your conclusion.

7. **Restate a key point in the conclusion, perhaps tying it to the Big Picture as well**. Be sure not to introduce more new information in the conclusion.

8. **Have an objective third party read it**. Ask someone else to read your article for clarity, meaning, and tone.

REMINDER

This might be the last official assignment you'll ever have that requires you to think specifically about your life purpose. You might be asked about an aspect of a career choice, strengths, skill sets, and the like, but few classes address this directly, and fewer still commit considerable time to it throughout the term.

Glossary

A

Academic Skills
Skills such as logic, critical reasoning, and reading, which are essential to all academic disciplines.

access point
The view, angle, or perspective at which you first interact with a person, situation, or piece of information.

Alfie Kohn Principle
The principle, based on the research of Alfie Kohn, that states that external rewards may bring about short-term extrinsic motivation, but they work against long-term intrinsic motivation.

assessment
An evaluation that reviews outcomes as well as inputs and helps determine a path for future action.

B

Big Picture Approach
A philosophy that encourages taking a broad view. This approach includes seeing things at the Brush-Stroke, Canvas, and Context Levels.

Brush-Stroke Level
The up-close view of something. At this level, you are close enough to see fine levels of detail.

C

Canvas Level
A view that is a bit farther back than the Brush-Stroke Level. At this level, you can see a fuller picture than you can at the closer Brush-Stroke Level.

cause
An ideal or goal pursued with passion and dedication. In most cases, a cause brings many people together to work toward shared goals, and those efforts in turn affect many others.

Communication Skills
Interpersonal and group skills that include speech, listening, interacting with others in conversation, social dialogue, small-group interaction, large-group interaction, mass communication, writing, and so on.

conceptualization
Putting our efforts into a broader perspective by pausing to take a step back, look at the big picture, and think about the desired outcomes of that journey so that we can better understand where we are in the context of where we're going.

Context Level
A view that enables you not only to see a full picture of the thing or situation at which you're looking but also to place it in a larger context.

Crossroads Principle
The principle that describes what happens when our formal learning and our informal experiences intersect, helping us make informed choices and internalize what we've learned.

D

deductive logic
The process of determining a specific conclusion based on general knowledge.

default
Something (such as a routine) that has evolved unintentionally over time.

design
To develop something (such as a routine) intentionally, through planning and decision making.

disposition
A mindset, outlook, or attitude; a tendency to exhibit a pattern of behavior directed toward a goal; sometimes called the "why" of learning.

Drum Principle
The principle that states that you need to pay serious attention to those tasks connected to a serious dream.

E

eureka moment
Derived from the Greek word "eureka," which translates as "I have found it!" today the word "eureka" indicates a discovery, especially an unexpected one, and a "eureka moment" has come to mean that instant when we find an answer someplace we never expected.

experiential learning
Learning gained from first-hand experience rather than from texts and lectures.

extrinsic motivation
A drive or reason behind actions and decisions that is inspired by external rewards or praise.

H

Herzberg Principle
The principle, based on the research of Frederick Herzberg, that states that removing dissatisfaction does not lead to intrinsic motivation.

I

Ideal Wedge
Your Life Wedge as you would like it to be, in an ideal future state.

ignoble cause
A cause that is generally acknowledged to be founded on dishonorable values and qualities.

immature dream
A dream about the future that is essentially wishful thinking, with no plan in place to support it.

inductive reasoning
The process of making a generalization based on specific knowledge.

intentional inquiry
A process of planned questioning; a routine that involves pausing at specific times or in specific circumstances to examine a situation, and then using specific, focused questions to process current information or gather new information.

intrinsic motivation
An internal drive or reason behind actions and decisions that reflects genuine interest.

K

knowledge
The category of learning that involves facts, formulas, dates, names, and so forth; sometimes called the "what" of learning.

L

lens
The perspective you hold that is determined by your personal circumstances or experiences, such as your job, academic specialization, or cultural background.

lifelong learning
An approach that emphasizes continual development and discovery of new ideas and information beyond college and throughout one's lifetime.

Life Wedge
A visual representation of the Wedge Principle, containing three elements: life purpose, life focus, and life gifts and life skills.

M

Mandela Principle
The principle, named after South African leader Nelson Mandela, that states, "No matter the length of the journey, perseverance is necessary to endure the struggle and reach the end. The right purpose makes perseverance possible."

mature dream
A dream that puts passion into action by developing the plans, strategies, skills, and resources needed to achieve it.

mission statement
A statement of purpose or declaration of intent that explains someone's or something's reason for being and avowed aims.

N

noble cause
A cause that is generally acknowledged to be founded on honorable values and qualities.

P

passive
An approach in which you sit back and allow things to happen to you.

personal alignment
When your actions match your words, and the choices you make are aligned with the dream you wish to pursue.

perspective
Literally, a point of view; in our discussions, it refers to seeing something at a different distance or from a different angle.

proactive
An approach in which you take the initiative to make things happen.

Proximity Principle
The idea that states it's difficult to read when you're too close to the page or to continue reading when you're too far from the story. A reminder of the need to maintain the right distance, or proximity, from what one is reading or learning.

purpose-guided learning
Learning that is directed and focused by a specific purpose or objective, such as a goal or mission statement.

R

Real Wedge
The Life Wedge that reflects how you're actually spending your time and prioritizing your energies right now.

RISE Model
A model used to respond to challenges, which includes the following steps: **Recognize** the reality of the challenge; **Identify** opportunities; **Strategize** a way forward; and **Execute** your strategy.

S

service learning
A type of experiential learning that involves helping another person or assisting a cause.

skills
The category of learning that involves mastery of techniques or application of knowledge; sometimes called the "how" of learning.

STIC Method
A routine that includes four distinct steps: stop, think, imagine, and commit.

syllogism
A three-line argument or logic form that serves as the basic deductive argument structure. In these arguments, the conclusion stems directly from two main facts (or premises).

T

Trade Skills
Also known as professional skills or skilled trades, these include a variety of learned techniques such as managing stock portfolios or welding.

V

values
Time-tested principles that help guide decisions and behavior.

vertigo
A phenomenon that induces a state of imbalance, often described as a sensation of dizziness or whirling around; frequently experienced by pilots.

W

waypower
The path toward a goal, by which the exertion of willpower helps you see opportunities and find resources and support.

Wedge Principle
The principle that states that just as a sharp, narrow wedge is more effective at splitting wood, a sharp, focused life is more effective at helping you reach your goals.

willpower
The personal strength and discipline, rooted in strong motivation, to carry out your decisions or plans.

Index

Note: Page numbers in *italics* indicate illustrations; page numbers followed by *n* indicate material in footnotes and source notes.